Sustainable Performance – A 30-Day Mindset Transformation Guide

Daily Lessons to Engineer Consistency, Prevent Burnout, and Sustain Results That Matter

Part of the *30-Day Mindset Transformation Series*

Other Books in the 30-Day Mindset Transformation Series

Reliability – A 30-Day Mindset Transformation Guide

Daily Lessons in Evidence-Based Thinking to Create a Reliability Mindset

---

Change & Culture – A 30-Day Mindset Transformation Guide

Daily Lessons Using the R3/R4 Change Model™ to Create a Shift in the Culture of Your Organization

---

Safety & Risk – A 30-Day Mindset Transformation Guide

Daily Lessons In Evidence-Based Safety: Merging Human Leadership and System Discipline

---

Problem-Solving – A 30-Day Mindset Transformation Guide

Daily Lessons in How to See Problems Differently and Develop More Effective Solutions

---

Communications – A 30-Day Mindset Transformation Guide

Daily Lessons to Reframe Communication as a Leadership Discipline, Not a Soft Skill

---

Abstract Thinking – A 30-Day Mindset Transformation Guide

Daily Lessons for Consuming and Translating Abstract Concepts into Actionable Meaning

Sustainable Performance – A 30-Day Mindset Transformation Guide

Daily Lessons to Engineer Consistency, Prevent Burnout, and Sustain Results That Matter

Andy Page, Ph.D.

Published by EBR Technologies

Sustainable Performance – A 30-Day Mindsets Transformation Guide

Copyright © 2025 EBR Technologies
All rights reserved. No part of this book may be reproduced, stored in a retrieval system, or transmitted in any form or by any means—electronic, mechanical, photocopying, recording, or otherwise—without prior written permission of the publisher.

ISBN: 979-8-9941269-0-5

Printed in the United States of America
Published by EBR Technologies

Sustainable Performance – A 30-Day Mindsets Transformation Guide

Disclaimer

This book is intended for educational and professional development purposes. The concepts, methods, and examples presented reflect the author's experience and interpretation of best practices within the fields of maintenance, reliability, and organizational culture.

While every effort has been made to ensure accuracy and clarity, the information provided is not a substitute for sound engineering judgment, professional advice, or site-specific analysis. Readers are encouraged to adapt these ideas to their own organizations responsibly, with appropriate technical validation and safety consideration.

Neither the author nor EBR Technologies, LLC assumes any responsibility for outcomes resulting from the application of the material in this book. All implementation decisions remain the sole responsibility of the reader and their organization.

Names and examples of companies, individuals, and situations have been used for illustrative purposes only and do not represent actual entities or events unless explicitly stated.

Sustainable Performance – A 30-Day Mindsets Transformation Guide

Table of Contents

Dedication 1
Abstract 2
Author's Note 3
Foreword 4
How to Use This 30-Day Guide 6
Why the Emphasis on Mindsets? 7
The Sustained Performance Framework 9
Day 1 — Execution Is an Operating System, Not a Personality Trait 16
Day 2 — A Slow Hit Is Still Faster Than Two Fast Misses 18
Day 3 — The Discipline of a Clean Start 20
Day 4 — Emotional Control Over Situational Noise 22
Day 5 — The Power of Cognitive Tempo 24
Day 6 — Matching Tempo to the Task and the Moment 26
Day 7 — Drift Happens Slowly — Catch It Early 28
Day 8 — Task-Line Focus: Narrow The Beam 30
Day 9 — Goal-Line Awareness: Never Lose Sight Of The Why 32
Day 10 —Identify What's Pulling You Off The Line 34
Day 11 — Eliminate Cognitive Switching 36
Day 12 — Jobs, Tasks, And Steps: Know The Difference 38
Day 13 — Attention To Detail Is A Reputation Multiplier 40
Day 14 — The Difference Between Motion And Progress 42
Day 15 — Not All Tasks Deserve Equal Cognitive Effort 44
Day 16 — The Cognitive Priority Matrix (Urgent Vs Important) 46
Day 17 — Cognitive Task Criticality: High vs. Standard vs. Low 48

Sustainable Performance – A 30-Day Mindsets Transformation Guide

Day 18 — The One-Decision Rule: Make Once, Apply Many 50
Day 19 — Familiarity Is the Slowest Teacher 52
Day 20 — Front-Loaded Learning Before the First Rep 54
Day 21 — Rehearsal Makes Performance Feel Familiar 56
Day 22 — A System Is Strongest Without Decision Fatigue 58
Day 23 — Reduce Friction, Increase Completion 60
Day 24 — Build the Environment That Matches the Identity 62
Day 25 — Cadence Beats Intensity 64
Day 26 — Small Cycles Are the Engine of Big Wins 66
Day 27 — Execution Strengthens Through Feedback, Not Memory . 68
Day 28 — Failure Is Not a Detour; It's the Data Stream 70
Day 29 — Create Confidence Through Transferable Performance.... 72
Day 30 — The Architecture Becomes the Identity 74
BONUS DAY — Building a Culture That Sustains Execution.......... 76
The Sustainable Performance Checklist 78
The Criticality & Priority Matrix 80
The PACE Builder Card 84
The Cognitive Gears Quick Card 88
When to Shift Gears 90
Cognitive Gear Principles 90
The Ten Signals of Cognitive Fatigue 92
The Drift Detection Guide 94
The Team Synchronization Protocol 98
About the Author 101
About EBR Technologies 102
Author's Note on the Use of AI 103

Sustainable Performance – A 30-Day Mindsets Transformation Guide

◆
───
◆

Sustainable Performance – A 30-Day Mindsets Transformation Guide

Dedication

For the people who understand that preparation is not optional.
For the ones who check their gear twice and verify the plan.
For those who refuse to show up any other way than…ready.

For the leaders who give clear direction, expect definitive execution,
and hold themselves to the same standard they demand.

For the teammates who carry their weight plus a little extra,
watch each other's blind spots,
and do the small things without being asked.

For the individuals who don't wait on motivation,
don't look for shortcuts,
and don't make excuses.

This book is for anyone committed to putting in the work,
to building systems that hold under pressure,
and to operating with discipline when it matters most.

Sustainable Performance – A 30-Day Mindsets Transformation Guide

Abstract

Sustainable performance is not the product of talent, motivation, or intensity—it is the outcome of systems that make consistent performance repeatable. This book challenges the common belief that reliable execution comes from personality or willpower or repetition that leads to familiarity, and instead demonstrates that high performance emerges from clarity, preparation, rhythm, and deliberate structure. Across thirty days, readers are introduced to a practical operating system built on front-loaded learning, environmental design, cognitive pacing, friction reduction, and feedback-driven improvement.

The framework presented here redefines execution as a process that can be engineered, practiced, and transferred across contexts. Through small cycles, steady cadence, and intentional habit architecture, individuals learn to shift from reactive effort to controlled, reproducible action. The book emphasizes that sustainable performance requires understanding the mechanisms behind focus, fatigue, drift, and recovery—while also reinforcing the leadership responsibilities of modeling discipline, aligning teams, and stabilizing culture.

By integrating cognitive science, operational principles, and field-tested practice, this guide provides a clear pathway for anyone seeking performance that lasts beyond the moment. Sustainable performance becomes less about trying harder and more about building systems that make the right actions the default—not the exception.

Sustainable Performance – A 30-Day Mindsets Transformation Guide

Author's Note

I didn't come to execution by accident.
From an early age, I noticed structure. I believed in patterns.
That belief is what pulled me toward manufacturing in the first place — the idea that outcomes weren't random, that quality wasn't luck, and that success could be engineered through repeatable processes. I trusted the logic of systems early on: if you understood the pattern, you could understand the problem; if you understood the problem, you could shape the outcome. That mindset has guided me my entire career.

What I didn't realize at first was how deeply that same principle applied to personal performance. I assumed people naturally followed structure, naturally built routines, naturally stabilized their own execution. Instead, I watched incredibly capable individuals struggle — not because they lacked talent, but because they lacked a system. I saw leaders pushed into chaos by unclear priorities, teams overwhelmed not by workload but by drift, and organizations relying on personality instead of process. It became obvious: human execution requires patterns just as much as machines do.

This book is the product of that realization. It captures the practices, design principles, and rhythms that make consistent performance possible — not just for manufacturing lines, but for people, leaders, and teams. These pages aren't about squeezing more effort out of yourself. They're about creating structure that removes friction, clarifies intent, and turns consistency into something you can rely on.

If there is one message I hope stays with you, it's this:
patterns don't limit performance — they unlock it.

— Andy Page, Ph.D.
Founder, EBR Technologies

Sustainable Performance – A 30-Day Mindsets Transformation Guide

Foreword

I've spent most of my career in environments where outcomes mattered long before opinions did. Manufacturing floors don't negotiate with you. Equipment doesn't care how you feel. Deadlines don't delay themselves. In those spaces, one truth becomes clear very quickly: patterns run the world, and if you don't understand the pattern, the pattern will run you.

What drew me into that world wasn't the machinery or the pace — it was the predictability. The precision. The logic that said, if the process is built well, the result will follow. I believed that from the beginning, long before I ever had the language for it. Systems made sense to me. Structure made sense to me.

Reproducibility made sense to me. It wasn't perfection I was chasing — it was reliability.

But the longer I worked with people, the more I noticed something surprising: many individuals were trying to execute their lives without the very thing they relied on at work.
- They wanted consistent performance without consistent structure.
- They wanted clarity without design.
- They wanted reliability while operating from improvisation.
- And they blamed themselves when it didn't work.

What I came to understand is that most people aren't inconsistent because they lack discipline — they're inconsistent because they're operating without a system. They think execution is a personality trait instead of an architecture. They try to compensate for missing structure with more effort, more intensity, and more pressure, which may work briefly but never sustainably.

This book exists to solve that problem.

Sustainable Performance – A 30-Day Mindsets Transformation Guide

Sustainable Performance is not about working harder. It's about building the internal and external systems that make consistency the default instead of the exception. It teaches you how to prepare, how to pace, how to rehearse, how to reduce friction, how to detect drift, how to protect your attention, and how to stabilize your performance under changing conditions. It is a framework for showing up the same way on a bad day as you do on a good one.

The world rewards people who can execute reliably.
    Organizations depend on them.
    Families trust them.
    Leaders rise because of them.
    Teams stabilize around them.

But reliability isn't a gift — it's a design.
It's a pattern you can build and strengthen over time.

My hope is that this book helps you construct that pattern with intention.
Not so you can do more, but so you can do what matters most — with clarity, calm, and confidence that doesn't evaporate when conditions change.

Because the future doesn't belong to the person with the most talent.
It belongs to the person with the most functional system.

Sustainable Performance — A 30-Day Mindsets Transformation Guide

How to Use This 30-Day Guide

This book is designed to be used, not read.
Think of it as a daily calibration tool — a short, structured reset that steadies your pace, sharpens your process, and reinforces the habits that make execution reliable.

Each day gives you one idea to apply immediately. Not theory. Not philosophy. A single operational upgrade you can test inside the next 24 hours. The goal is simple: improve your system a little at a time until consistency becomes automatic.

Don't multitask with these entries.
Open the book, read one day, and decide how you will run that idea during the next block of your work. The value doesn't come from the page — it comes from the rep. **Sustainable performance** is repetition by design: small cycles, clean resets, predictable gains.

Each entry follows the same structure:

- **The Lesson** — A practical shift in how to build, run, or strengthen your execution system.
- **The Reflection** — A short diagnostic to help you see the patterns driving your results.
- **The Commitment** — A clear behavioral anchor for the next cycle.
- **The EBR Principle** — A field-truth that reinforces why the system works.

Treat the book as a 30-day field test of your own operating system.
You are not memorizing concepts — you are building architecture.
Run each day cleanly. Evaluate. Adjust. Repeat.
By the end, you won't just understand **sustainable performance** — you'll be living it.

Sustainable Performance – A 30-Day Mindsets Transformation Guide

Why the Emphasis on Mindsets?

Every improvement journey begins with a decision — and every decision begins with a mindset. Before you can change what people do, you have to change what they believe about what matters. That's why every book in this series starts with thinking, not tools. Procedures and policies don't stick if the people inside the system still see the world the same way.

Mindset is the hidden architecture of behavior — the lens through which we interpret data, make judgments, and justify choices. When the frame is wrong, the evidence doesn't matter. Leaders often install new methods on top of old mindsets, then wonder why the change collapses. Methods manage behavior. Mindsets determine it.

If you want different results, you must start upstream — with how people think about their work, their role, and their responsibility.

Mindset as the Bridge Between Human and System

Reliable organizations understand that mindset is the bridge between human leadership and system discipline. Systems give structure; mindsets give meaning. One without the other drifts.

Checks, audits, and communication loops only work when people believe the discipline itself matters. When people see safety or reliability as compliance, they work to avoid blame. When they see it as stewardship, they work to protect value. The process may look identical — but the mindset behind it changes everything.

Belief Before Behavior

Human performance research shows that people act their way into consistency, but believe their way into commitment. Beliefs shape what we notice, how we interpret risk, and what we feel responsible to do.

Change efforts built only on process often trigger resistance. When they begin with mindset, they invite reflection instead of defensiveness. Mindset work slows us down long enough to see our thinking — and once we can see it, we can choose it.

The Role of Reflection

Each day in this series uses reflection because reflection turns belief into evidence. It's easy to agree with a principle; it's harder to see where our own behavior quietly violates it.

The daily structure — The Moment, The Mindset, The Discipline, Reflection, Commitment — surfaces that gap. The goal is not guilt; it's growth. Real change comes from small, repeated recalibrations — a rhythm of awareness.

Evidence-Based Thinking

Mindset work is also evidence work. It replaces assumption with observation and story with pattern. When you treat your own reactions as data, you become both scientist and subject.

Evidence-based leaders look for behavioral patterns and adjust beliefs to match reality. These pages don't give rules; they offer mirrors — invitations to see clarity, consistency, or drift in your own environment.

The Outcome

When mindsets change, everything aligns faster. Communication sharpens. Systems gain purpose. Results finally match intent.

Mindset isn't the warm-up to the work — it *is* the work. It's how you close the gap between what you say and what you show. When leaders change how they think, they don't just create new systems — they create new possibilities.

The Sustained Performance Framework

A Model for Repeatable, Reliable, Mission-Grade Performance

1. The Identity Layer — What You Believe About Execution

This layer shapes the mindset you bring to every task.

1.1 Execution Is an Operating System, Not a Personality Trait

- Execution is not energy, charisma, motivation, or temperament.
- It is architecture: systems you run, not moods you ride.

1.2 Consistency Is the Byproduct of Structure, Not Desire

- People rarely fail from laziness; they fail from operating without a system.
- Rhythm beats motivation.
- Predictability comes from engineered habits.

1.3 Front-Loaded Learning Creates Early Fluency (Integration Point #1)

- Relying on familiarity assumes you'll see the task often enough to stumble into competence.
- But frequency is not guaranteed, and trial-and-error is too slow.
- Mastery begins before the reps—through deliberate study, previewing, simulation, mental rehearsal, and structured walk-throughs.
- You don't wait for repetition to teach you; you teach yourself before repetition even arrives.

2. The Cognitive Layer — How You Think Before You Act

2.1 Clarity Before Velocity
You cannot execute what you cannot articulate.

2.2 Codification of Situations
- The mind works faster and cleaner when information is grouped.
- You sort the situation into categories, patterns, and known structures.
- You ask: *What is this?* before *What do I do about it?*

2.3 Criticality Awareness
- Every situation contains layers of importance.
- Not everything deserves equal attention.
- Identify the vital, ignore the ornamental.

2.4 Familiarity vs. Front-Loaded Learning (Integration Point #2)
This is the deeper psychological architecture:

Familiarity
- Slow acquisition
- Dependent on exposure frequency
- Vulnerable to forgetting
- Highly situational
- Produces uneven performance

Front-Loaded Learning
- Fast acquisition
- Independent of repetition
- Builds competence before contact
- Creates smoother execution under pressure
- Reduces early-phase error rates
- Shifts learning from accidental → intentional

Core Principle Added: *Execution improves in proportion to how much of the learning happens ahead of the doing.*

3. The Structural Layer — The Systems You Run

Execution becomes sustainable when the system outlives the moment.

3.1 Pre-Planning Systems
- Mission clarity
- Task decomposition
- Prioritization logic
- Time boxing

3.2 Gear Preparation (The 1/3–1/3–1/3 Rule)
- 1/3 planning
- 1/3 gear prep
- 1/3 rehearsal
- Gear includes tools, clothing, environment, documentation, digital files, mental readiness, emotional posture.

3.3 Front-Loaded Learning as a System (Integration Point #3)

Front-loading becomes part of the planning discipline:
- Briefing
- Study packets
- Pre-reads
- Technical previews
- Mental simulations
- Role-play
- Decision trees

This turns early performance from fragile → stable.

4. The Behavioral Layer — What You Actually Do in the Moment

4.1 One-Touch Rule
Reduce rework by completing a task the first time it's in your hands.

4.2 A Slow Hit Is Still Faster Than Two Fast Misses
- Precision > speed.
- A clean, well-aimed attempt beats rushed multi-failure cycles.

4.3 Rehearsal Over Familiarity (Integration Point #4)
Rehearsal is the behavioral expression of front-loaded learning.
- Dry runs
- Cue-carding
- Walk-throughs
- Muscle-memory tightening
- Micro-practice

You enter the task already warm.

5. The Rhythmic Layer — Sustained performance Over Time

5.1 Cadence Over Intensity
- Daily discipline beats sporadic bursts.
- Small, structured cycles > inconsistent surges.

5.2 Checkpoints Replace Hope
- Measurement
- After-action reviews
- Adjustment cycles

5.3 Repetition Reinforces What Was Front-Loaded (Integration Point #5)
You don't practice to *learn it for the first time.*
You practice to *strengthen what you already understand.*

Familiarity becomes reinforcement rather than your primary teacher.

6. The Environmental Layer — How You Shape the Conditions

6.1 Reduce Friction
Lower the activation energy required to start tasks.

6.2 Engineer the Workspace for Predictability
- Tools visible
- Pathways clear
- Materials pre-staged

6.3 Make the Default Easy, and the Wrong Path Hard
Design wins over willpower.

6.4 Build Environments That Support Front-Loaded Learning (Integration Point #6)
- Visual cues
- Ready-reference cards
- Shared mental models
- Standard briefings
- Templates
- Playbooks
- Checklists

The environment becomes a cognitive multiplier.

7. The Feedback Layer — The Loop That Never Stops

7.1 Real-Time Corrections

Rapid micro-adjustments beat heroic effort.

7.2 Post-Event Learning

Structured reviews replace guesswork.

7.3 Failure Is Data

Not embarrassment.
Not indictment.
Not narrative.
Just information.

7.4 Front-Loaded Learning Accelerates Future Cycles (Integration Point #7)

Because you learn deliberately before the event, each feedback loop builds on an already-structured mental framework.
Meaning:

- You improve faster.
- Your corrections are more accurate.
- Your next execution cycle is smoother.

Summary of Integration Points

To make it explicit, the Familiarity vs. Front-Loaded Learning concept is now embedded across seven places in the framework:

1. **Identity Layer:** Fluency begins before reps.
2. **Cognitive Layer:** Familiarity is accidental; front-loading is intentional.
3. **Structural Layer:** Added as a system inside planning.
4. **Behavioral Layer:** Rehearsal is the action form of front-loading.
5. **Rhythmic Layer:** Repetition reinforces, not teaches.
6. **Environmental Layer:** Build cues that support front-loading.
7. **Feedback Layer:** Faster learning because the mind had structure beforehand.

Sustainable Performance – A 30-Day Mindsets Transformation Guide

Day 1 — Execution Is an Operating System, Not a Personality Trait

The Lesson

Execution gets mislabeled as a personality trait far too often. People talk about it as if some individuals were simply born "doers" while others weren't. But real, sustained performance has nothing to do with temperament. It has everything to do with architecture. It is the operating system running underneath every choice you make—quiet, invisible, but determinative. It dictates how you prioritize, how you navigate uncertainty, and how reliably you follow through once the spark of motivation burns off. Systems outperform personality for one reason: systems don't care about your mood. They convert responsibility into rhythm, and rhythm into predictability.

Inconsistency, for most people, is not a moral failure. It isn't laziness, and it isn't lack of desire. It's the unavoidable result of trying to perform without structure. When you rely on memory instead of method, or motivation instead of design, your performance becomes hostage to whatever the day decides to hand you. A system frees you from that randomness. It gives you an anchor—clarity about what matters, sequencing so it happens in the right order, and checkpoints so nothing quietly slips off the radar. Structure doesn't restrict your life; it stabilizes it. It turns chaos into something you can actually manage.

And here's the shift that changes everything: when you treat execution as something you run instead of something you are, you reclaim control. Systems can be upgraded. Workflows can be redesigned. Habits can be rewritten. Friction points can be eliminated. Suddenly, discipline is not something you chase—it's something your environment produces. Sustained performance stops depending on willpower and starts flowing from intentional design. And once the design is in place, momentum becomes easier to start, easier to sustain, and far easier to repeat day after day.

Sustainable Performance – A 30-Day Mindsets Transformation Guide

The Reflection

Think about the parts of your life where you perform well without struggle. Chances are, those successes aren't powered by personality—they're powered by structure. These areas already have rhythms, routines, or rules that make execution almost automatic. This is the quiet advantage of a good operating system: it removes the need for constant decision-making.

Now contrast that with the areas where you feel reactive, scattered, or inconsistent. Those are the places where you are relying on motivation instead of method. They feel harder not because you're less capable, but because the system beneath them is missing or incomplete.

Finally, reflect on how much stress could be removed if the right structure existed. How many tasks would feel lighter? How many goals would feel more achievable? Sustained performance begins the moment you stop blaming personality and start building systems.

The Commitment

- I will stop treating execution as a personality problem.
- I will identify one area where a system is missing and begin designing it.
- I will replace motivation-dependence with method-dependence.
- I will treat structure as the foundation of performance.

EBR Principle — Systems Create Consistency

Predictability is engineered, not discovered.

Sustainable Performance – A 30-Day Mindsets Transformation Guide

Day 2 — A Slow Hit Is Still Faster Than Two Fast Misses

The Lesson

Most communication failures aren't the result of a lack of intelligence, talent, or even intention—they're the result of moving too quickly. People rush to send a message, rush to close the loop, rush to "get it off their plate," and in that speed they trade accuracy for activity. The result is predictable: they miss the mark, correct themselves, miss again, explain the confusion, and only then finally hit the target. By the time understanding finally lands, the team has spent more time untangling the mess than they would have spent doing it carefully the first time.

A slow hit is still faster than two fast misses. Leaders forget this because speed feels productive. Speed *appears* decisive. But speed without accuracy creates rework—communication's most expensive tax. When you slow down long enough to choose the right words, shape the right context, and anticipate the likely points of misinterpretation, you reduce the number of cycles required to transfer understanding. That "slowness" pays back immediately in clarity, alignment, and execution.

Communicating deliberately is not the same as communicating slowly. Deliberate communication is intentional, structured, and engineered to land on the first pass. It trades a few extra seconds on the front end for hours of avoided confusion on the back end. It is the discipline of pausing long enough to be understood—not just heard. And in environments where uncertainty is costly and misinterpretation is dangerous, that pause is not optional. It is leadership.

The Reflection

Where in the last week did speed create rework for you? Think about the update, the direction, or the explanation that had to be repeated, clarified, or corrected. Most leaders underestimate how often this happens.

Now consider the opposite: the times when you slowed down long enough to communicate clearly. How much smoother did execution become afterward?

The Commitment

- I will choose clarity over speed.
- I will engineer messages that land on the first pass.
- I will avoid rework by slowing down at the start.
- I will treat communication as a precision task, not a speed drill.

EBR Principle — Precision Before Pace

Understanding delivered once is always faster than misunderstanding delivered twice.

Sustainable Performance – A 30-Day Mindsets Transformation Guide

Day 3 — The Discipline of a Clean Start

The Lesson

A clean start is not *just* about neatness. Neatness of appearance, a made bed, a clear desk, organized tools, a swept workspace—these aren't trivial chores. They are the **micro-disciplines that convert your environment from passive noise into active support**. When the little things in your world are already handled, your mind doesn't waste energy carrying them. Cognitive load drops. Focus rises. And before the first task even begins, you've built a runway instead of cluttering one.

High performance begins with high readiness, and readiness is engineered long before the day actually starts. A clean start is the discipline of setting the conditions for execution. When you reset your space, stage your gear, straighten your appearance, or check your tools, you are not performing cosmetic order—you are performing mental alignment. You are telling your mind, *"These small details will not compete with the mission today."* That single decision preserves attention, reduces friction, and sharpens the first hour of your day into a real advantage.

And momentum matters. Clean starts build clean actions; clean actions build clean decisions; clean decisions build clean days. People underestimate how quickly the early minutes can tip the whole day forward or backward. A scattered morning forces your brain into recovery mode; a clean start places it in control. Over time, this compounds: fewer rushed errors, fewer emotional overreactions, fewer avoidable frustrations. A clean start isn't perfectionism—it's preparation. And preparation is what makes discipline sustainable instead of exhausting. Start clean, and the rest of the day follows suit.

Sustainable Performance – A 30-Day Mindsets Transformation Guide

The Reflection

Think back to the days that felt heavier than they should have. How often did they begin with disorganization, clutter, or mental noise? A scattered start raises your cognitive load before you've done a single meaningful thing. It forces your mind to solve problems it shouldn't have to, and that drag follows you into every decision.

Now think of the mornings you began with order and intention. The days when your space was ready, your gear was staged, your appearance was squared away, and the little things were already resolved. You felt calmer, clearer, and more capable—not because the work was easier, but because *you* were more prepared to meet it.

If a clean start is one of the simplest ways to reduce friction and increase readiness, what would change if you treated it as non-negotiable?

The Commitment

- I will begin with clarity, order, and intention.
- I will handle the small things early so they do not tax my attention later.
- I will protect the first moments of the day as the foundation of high readiness.
- I will start clean so I can perform clean.

EBR Principle

High performance begins with high readiness—and readiness begins with a clean start.

Day 4 — Emotional Control Over Situational Noise

The Lesson

Emotional control is not the absence of emotion — it's the ability to keep emotion from being **hijacked** by the noise of the moment. Most people think they get derailed by big events, but high performers know the truth: it's the small, unexpected disruptions that knock you off rhythm. A late email. A sharp comment. A change in schedule. A glance, a tone, a misunderstanding. These little ripples create situational noise, and if you're not careful, that noise becomes internalized. Once your emotions start reacting to the environment instead of steering it, the day stops being something you execute and becomes something that happens *to* you.

Emotional control is the discipline of **separating the signal from the noise**. Not everything requires a reaction. Not everything deserves your energy. And not everything that feels urgent is actually important. High performers learn to create a buffer between stimulus and response — a pause that prevents overreaction, misinterpretation, or escalation. That pause is where clarity lives. Without it, you become entangled in the moment, and your emotional state becomes a mirror of whatever chaos you walk through. With it, you remain steady, intentional, and aligned with your mission, not the momentary turbulence around you.

This discipline becomes even more important when you're pursuing sustained performance. Situational noise drains cognitive bandwidth, raises stress hormones, narrows perspective, and pushes you into reactive patterns. Emotional control restores that bandwidth. It widens your field of view. It keeps your decisions clean and your tempo stable. It transforms interruptions from threats into manageable variables. Over time, this is one of the hidden superpowers of high performers: the ability to stay composed when everyone else is bending toward the noise. Emotional control isn't calmness — it's command.

The Reflection

Think about the moments when you felt thrown off your game. Was it truly the size of the event, or was it the suddenness of it? How often did small disruptions create an emotional ripple that changed the tone of your entire day? Situational noise is subtle — and that's why it's powerful.

Now think of the times you maintained control despite the noise. You paused, breathed, recalibrated. The moment didn't take you with it; you stayed anchored. That's not luck — that's discipline. What would happen if that level of control became your default instead of your exception?

The Commitment

- I will pause before reacting.
- I will protect my emotional state from the noise of the moment.
- I will stay anchored to intention, not turbulence.
- I will remain steady, deliberate, and in command.

EBR Principle

Emotional control turns situational noise into manageable variables — not drivers of your day.

Day 5 — The Power of Cognitive Tempo

The Lesson

Every performer — in sports, leadership, craftsmanship, aviation, or operations — has a cognitive tempo, a personal rhythm that determines the speed and quality of their decisions. Most people never discover theirs. They move at the speed of the environment, the speed of their inbox, the speed of other people's urgency. Their thinking is reactive, their pace inconsistent, and their execution scattered. High performers operate differently. They understand that **the rhythm you choose becomes the rhythm you impose** — on conversations, on meetings, on decisions, and on outcomes.

Cognitive tempo is the internal metronome that shapes your clarity. Move too fast and you lose precision. Move too slow and you lose opportunity. But when your tempo is intentional, you create a cadence that supports clean thinking: your breathing steadies, your focus narrows, and your actions line up behind the mission instead of the moment. It is not simply "working at your own pace." It is selecting the pace that best fits the complexity of the task, the stakes of the decision, and the conditions you're operating in. Your tempo becomes an act of leadership — both over yourself and over the situation.

This is why high performers guard their cognitive tempo so fiercely. They know that interruptions are inevitable, but tempo loss is optional. When you allow the environment to dictate your speed, you surrender your advantage. When you maintain your rhythm, you set the standard for everyone around you. Teams feel calmer. Conversations sharpen. Problems unfold more logically. And you regain control of your mental bandwidth. Cognitive tempo is not simply about speed — it is about **commanding the pace at which you think, decide, and execute.** When you master your tempo, you master your day.

Sustainable Performance – A 30-Day Mindsets Transformation Guide

The Reflection

Consider the times when your day felt chaotic. Was the problem really the volume of work — or was it the speed at which you were pushed to operate? Now think of the moments when you deliberately slowed down, took a breath, clarified your next step, and regained control. Your thinking sharpened instantly. Your decisions improved. Your stress dropped.

Your tempo is one of the most powerful tools you have. What would change if you chose it on purpose instead of inheriting it from the environment?

The Commitment

Today, I will set my own cognitive rhythm.
I will not allow urgency or noise to dictate my speed.
I will match my tempo to the level of thinking the moment requires.
I will lead with clarity, not momentum.

EBR Principle

Your tempo sets the standard — for your mind, your decisions, and the environment around you.

Day 6 — Matching Tempo to the Task and the Moment

The Lesson

Every task carries its own natural rhythm, and high performers learn to match their tempo to the moment rather than forcing the moment to match their tempo. Most people operate at a default speed—too fast when clarity is needed, too slow when decisiveness matters. This mismatch creates friction, mistakes, and emotional churn. But when you choose your pace deliberately, your thinking becomes cleaner, your movements smoother, and your execution more reliable.

This is the deeper truth behind the phrase **"Slow is smooth and smooth is fast."** It isn't about literally moving slowly; it's about **stabilizing your process so your actions flow cleanly**. Slow creates smoothness by preventing rushed errors. Smooth creates fast by eliminating rework, confusion, and correction. When you match your tempo to the complexity and stakes of the task, you build this stability on purpose. Strategic thinking requires slowing down. Technical precision requires steady rhythm. Crisis response requires rapid, controlled action. The skill is not speed — the skill is *tempo selection*.

The real advantage comes when you can shift gears without losing control. Tempo adaptation is not reactive; it's intentional. You slow down to reduce error rates. You accelerate to seize momentum. You hold steady to maintain clarity under pressure. This adaptability prevents you from being pulled into the chaos of the moment or trapped in hesitation. It expands your operational bandwidth and turns you into someone who is consistently composed, precise, and ready to respond at the right speed — not just any speed.

The Reflection

When was the last time you moved too fast and paid for it with a preventable mistake? When was the last time you moved too slowly and missed an opening? These mismatches often go unnoticed, but they accumulate into stress, rework, and frustration.

Now recall the moments when you slowed down intentionally, got smooth, and everything flowed. Or the moments you accelerated decisively and created momentum. That wasn't luck — that was the right tempo meeting the right moment. What would change if you made that level of control the norm?

The Commitment

- I will set my pace with intention.
- I will slow down when clarity matters and accelerate when the path is clean.
- I will choose smoothness over rush, precision over panic, rhythm over noise.
- I will respond at the speed the moment deserves.

EBR Principle

Slow creates smooth. Smooth creates fast. Matching tempo creates mastery.

Sustainable Performance – A 30-Day Mindsets Transformation Guide

Day 7 — Drift Happens Slowly — Catch It Early

The Lesson

Most performance failures do not begin with a major mistake. They begin with a small drift — a slight slip in attention, a minor shortcut, a casual lapse in discipline. Drift rarely announces itself. It begins quietly, hides in the margins, and grows through accumulation. A skipped preparation step. A rushed decision. A relaxed standard. A moment of emotional indulgence. None of these feel dangerous in isolation, but over time, they compound. By the time drift becomes visible, it has already shaped your day, your habits, and your outcomes.

High performers understand that drift is not a crisis to react to — it is a signal to detect early. Drift shows up first in the small things: clutter creeping onto the desk, impatience creeping into your tone, inconsistency creeping into your tempo. The earlier you catch these shifts, the easier they are to correct. This is why readiness matters. This is why cognitive tempo matters. This is why emotional control matters. Each discipline protects you from the tiny deviations that slowly pull you away from clean execution. Catching drift is not about perfection; it is about maintaining alignment before misalignment becomes momentum.

The power of catching drift early is that it prevents overcorrection. When you wait too long, you don't just fix the issue — you have to fight the momentum behind it. But when you spot drift in the first inch instead of the first mile, course correction is smooth, quick, and almost effortless. Early detection saves energy, preserves focus, and protects your day from unraveling. Drift is inevitable; the discipline is catching it before it turns into drag. High performers don't just work hard — they stay aligned.

The Reflection

Think back to the days that went sideways. Did they fall apart suddenly, or did they drift off course slowly? What small lapses showed up early — in preparation, in emotion, in attention — that you didn't catch until they had grown? Drift almost always begins with something small.

Now consider the times you noticed a slip early and corrected it before it spread. A quick reset. A small adjustment. A brief moment of self-awareness. How much smoother did the rest of the day feel? What would your performance look like if you caught drift consistently at the first signal, not the fifth?

The Commitment

- I will watch for the small shifts that signal drift.
- I will correct early instead of waiting for misalignment to build.
- I will guard my standards before they slip, not after.
- I will stay aligned, steady, and intentional.

EBR Principle

Drift is inevitable. Early correction is optional — and that's where performance is won.

Day 8 — Task-Line Focus: Narrow The Beam

The Lesson

There is a moment in every high-stakes environment—military, manufacturing, aviation, sports—when the performer must narrow their field of view to the single task directly in front of them. Everything else becomes background noise. This is Task-Line Focus, and it is the first half of what will become your Week 2 discipline: executing the present step with precision while the mission hums quietly in your peripheral mind.

Task-Line Focus is not the same as multitasking or effort stacking. It is the discipline of making your world small on purpose—shrinking your attention down to what the task actually requires, not what the day is demanding. Sustainable performance begins here, because overwhelm is usually not volume—it is diffusion. When your awareness leaks into ten different directions, your performance fractures into ten incomplete efforts. Narrow the beam and the entire system stabilizes.

But narrowing the beam requires courage. It means letting go of what you cannot influence in this moment. It means trusting that the mission, the outcome, the long arc of the work will still be there when you complete the next step. Sustainable performers do not sprint mentally. They aim their cognitive flashlight at the exact square foot of work that matters **right now**, and they execute that square foot fully before they move the beam.

Over time, this creates a pattern: fewer errors, fewer mental resets, fewer restarts, and dramatically more consistency. Systems thrive when the human at the center stops scattering and starts aiming. Narrow the beam, and both your clarity and your control rise sharply.

Sustainable Performance – A 30-Day Mindsets Transformation Guide

The Reflection

Where does your attention naturally drift when you're working? Toward the future? Toward the noise? Toward everything at once? Task-Line Focus asks you to reclaim the present square inch of responsibility. Think about one task today where narrowing your beam would have changed the quality of the result. What made it hard to stay present? What pulled you off the line? What would it have taken to stay with the task until it was complete?

Sustainable performance is not about intensity—it's about intentionality. When you narrow the beam, you build the muscle of deliberate focus. And deliberate focus is how you steer your days instead of being pulled through them.

The Commitment

- I will make my world small when I am performing a task.
- I will give one task my undivided attention until it reaches a clean stopping point.
- I will notice when my beam widens unintentionally and pull it back on purpose.
- I will practice Task-Line Focus as the foundation for focused-performance until it feels comfortable to do.

EBR Principle

A scattered mind produces scattered results; a narrowed beam produces deliberate, repeatable execution.

Day 9 — Goal-Line Awareness: Never Lose Sight Of The Why

The Lesson

If Day 8 taught you to narrow the beam, Day 9 teaches you not to narrow it so much that you forget why the beam is pointed there in the first place. Task-Line Focus gives you precision; Goal-Line Awareness gives you direction. Sustainable performance requires both, because precision without purpose is just well-organized drift.

Goal-Line Awareness is the skill of keeping the *why* of the work alive in the background of your mind—not loud, not distracting, but always present. It is the constant, steady hum of mission intent. When you know the purpose behind what you're doing, decisions become easier, trade-offs become clearer, and your sense of urgency calibrates itself naturally. Purpose isn't motivational fluff; it's cognitive architecture. It organizes your effort.

When people lose sight of the goal line, they begin to work mechanically. Tasks become boxes to check rather than levers that move outcomes. Energy drops. Attention fades. Errors increase because context collapses. But when the goal line is visible—even faintly—it influences your posture, your tempo, and your judgment. It reminds you that every task is connected to something larger. Sustainable performers never let that connection go dark.

This discipline also keeps you from being seduced by the wrong urgencies. Just because something demands attention doesn't mean it deserves it. Goal-Line Awareness is what tells you whether the noise in front of you actually moves the mission or merely interrupts it. Without this layer of awareness, you can execute flawlessly on items that do not matter. With it, you stay aligned, efficient, and intentional.

The Reflection

Where did your attention go today—toward the work or toward the purpose behind the work? Think of a moment when you slipped into Task-Line autopilot and forgot the mission you were supposed to be advancing. What shifted when purpose faded? How did it affect your energy, your decisions, or the quality of your actions?

Goal-Line Awareness is not about being lofty or philosophical. It is about directing effort with accuracy. Sit with this: How much of your stress comes from a lack of clarity about your true goal line—and how much ease would return if that line were visible again?

The Commitment

- I will keep the purpose of my work visible, even while executing the smallest task.
- I will check my direction before I check the next item off my list.
- I will not let urgency override intention.
- I will stay aware of the goal line that gives meaning to today's effort.

EBR Principle

Purpose steadies the mind; when the goal line stays visible, the work finds its direction.

Day 10 —Identify What's Pulling You Off The Line

The Lesson

Execution fails more often from friction than fatigue. It's not the big obstacles that break your rhythm—it's the small, silent drags that slowly pull you off the line. A buzzing notification, an unfinished thought, a cluttered desk corner, a vague instruction, a person hovering at the edge of your attention… none of these seem fatal alone. But together, they grind the edges of your focus until precision fades and drift begins.

The Friction Test is the discipline of noticing what steals two percent of your attention at a time. Sustainable performers don't wait until friction becomes failure—they detect the micro-interference early and clear it before it compounds. Think of a machinist who stops to wipe debris from a bearing surface: it takes seconds, but it prevents hours of damage. Your mind works the same way. A single pebble in your cognitive shoe seems trivial until your gait has been altered for half the day.

Friction doesn't usually announce itself. It shows up as small delays, unnecessary re-starts, repeated corrections, or that mild feeling of "Why is this taking longer than it should?" The moment execution starts to feel heavier than the size of the task, friction is present. And here's the danger: when friction goes unrecognized, people start blaming themselves, not the drag. They try harder instead of lighter. They push more instead of clearing the interference.

Sustainable performance is not about grinding through resistance—it's about eliminating the resistance that never should have been there in the first place. When you run the Friction Test deliberately—pause, observe, name the drag, remove it—you restore flow, precision, and stability far faster than by simply adding more effort.

The Reflection

Where did friction show up in your work today? Was it noise, clutter, confusion, disorganization, or someone else's urgency bleeding into your space? Think of one moment where the task should have been straightforward but wasn't. What pulled you off the line? What tiny drag did you tolerate instead of clearing?

The Friction Test is awareness training. Once you learn to see friction early, you begin to protect your clarity instinctively. And that skill turns average days into high-control days—without adding an ounce of extra effort.

The Commitment

- I will pause when a task feels heavier than it should and look for friction.
- I will remove small drags before they become large delays.
- I will guard my attention by eliminating hidden interference, not by pushing harder against it.
- I will treat friction as a signal, not a flaw.

EBR Principle

Small drags create big deviations; clear the friction early and your execution stays true.

Day 11 — Eliminate Cognitive Switching

The Lesson

One of the greatest threats to sustainable performance is not distraction—it's switching. Cognitive switching is the mental gear-shift you perform every time you jump from one thought, task, or urgency to another. It feels productive because it feels fast. But every switch has a hidden cost: the time it takes your mind to recalibrate, reload context, and reorient to a new objective.

The danger is that the cost is invisible. When you switch tasks five, ten, or twenty times an hour, you don't notice each re-entry delay. But they accumulate. And as they accumulate, precision drops, errors increase, and the quality of your thinking erodes. What looks like a busy day is often just a scattered one. And scattered days never create sustainable performance—they create fatigue disguised as accomplishment.

Eliminating cognitive switching doesn't mean reducing your responsibilities; it means reducing your internal fragmentation. It means sequencing your work instead of scattering it. It means protecting the mental "loading screen" that comes with every new task, so you aren't constantly rebooting your brain. When you focus on one task until it reaches a clean stop point, you eliminate the cognitive tax that switching silently charges.

Sustainable performers learn to feel the moment just before a switch—when attention begins to tilt, when impulse reaches for something else, when noise pulls the mind sideways. That's the critical moment. If you can hold the line in that precise second, the entire trajectory of the task changes. Work becomes cleaner, thinking becomes sharper, and your mental endurance increases dramatically. What you're really eliminating is waste—mental waste that steals your best clarity without your permission.

The Reflection

Where did you switch today? And more importantly—why? Was it boredom, impulse, panic, curiosity, or someone else's urgency? Think back to a task you kept leaving and re-entering. How much time did the re-entry cost you? What pieces had to be reloaded each time?

Eliminating switching is not about being rigid. It's about letting your brain operate at its natural efficiency, without being continually disrupted by your own impulses. Notice the moment before your next switch. What would it take to stay with the task just a little longer?

The Commitment

- I will work tasks to clean stop points before shifting to something else.
- I will recognize the moment just before a switch and steady my attention.
- I will sequence my work intentionally instead of scattering it impulsively.
- I will protect my mind from unnecessary context resets.

EBR Principle

Every switch steals clarity; stay with the task long enough for your mind to do its best work.

Day 12 — Jobs, Tasks, And Steps: Know The Difference

The Lesson

Confusion creates drag. And one of the most common forms of confusion in execution is the quiet mixing of jobs, tasks, and steps. When these three layers blur together, you lose precision. You misjudge effort. You overestimate or underestimate what's required. And your ability to sequence work collapses into a vague sense of "I just need to get this done."

A **job** is the whole mission: the beginning, middle, and end of a piece of work. A job has an outcome. It has a finish line. A job answers the question, *What are we trying to accomplish?*

A **task** is a major component of that job. A task is a chunk of work large enough to carry meaning but small enough to manage. Tasks break the job into logical, workable segments. A task answers the question, *What must happen to move the job forward?*

A **step** is the smallest actionable unit of execution. It is one motion, one action, one discrete thing a person must perform. Steps answer the question, *What do I do next?*

Sustainable performance requires clean separation between these layers because your brain handles each one differently. Jobs require clarity. Tasks require structure. Steps require focus. When you treat a job like a step, you overwhelm yourself. When you treat a step like a job, you overcomplicate it. And when you treat a task like neither, you drift between extremes—too vague to be precise, too detailed to be effective.

Mastering this distinction gives you control over your tempo. It prevents you from switching too early or lingering too long. It allows you to plan at the right altitude and execute at the right granularity. When you know whether you're working a job, a task, or a step, you automatically know how to think and how much attention to apply.

The Reflection

Where did you blur these layers today? Did you treat a full job like a single step and then feel overwhelmed? Or did you get trapped inside a tiny step and forget the larger task it belonged to? Think of one piece of work that felt heavier than expected—was the weight coming from the work itself or from the layer you were operating at?

When you choose the correct layer, your mind relaxes. Work becomes navigable. And the confusion that once felt like complexity reveals itself as nothing more than poor categorization.

The Commitment

- I will identify whether I'm working at the job, task, or step level.
- I will think at the altitude that matches the work in front of me.
- I will break jobs into tasks and tasks into steps before I begin.
- I will not let blurred layers create artificial overwhelm.

EBR Principle

Right work at the right layer keeps execution clean, calm, and controllable.

Day 13 — Attention To Detail Is A Reputation Multiplier

The Lesson

Most people think attention to detail is about perfectionism. It isn't. Attention to detail is about **credibility**. It's about the quiet signals you send through the quality of your work—signals that tell others whether they can trust you, rely on you, and build something with you over time. Details are not ornamental; they are diagnostic. They reveal whether you operate with intention or inconsistency.

In sustainable performance, details are the first place drift appears and the first place discipline is proven. A misaligned number, a sloppy summary, a missing tool, a small delay, an unchecked assumption—none of these failures is catastrophic on its own. But they accumulate. And as they accumulate, they begin to shape how people interpret your capability. Not because they judge the error, but because they sense the pattern.

Every detail you handle well reinforces confidence. Every detail you dismiss weakens it. Over time, this compounds into reputation—either as someone whose work people don't have to double-check, or someone whose work always seems to need a second look. Sustainable performers aim for the former, not by obsessing, but by caring. They respect the fact that every detail is a piece of the system and that the system is stronger when its pieces are right.

Attention to detail also influences your tempo. When you handle details early, they don't become disruptions later. When you miss them, they show up as friction, rework, and frustration at the worst possible moment. Sustainable performance demands that you treat details not as afterthoughts but as stabilizers—small calibrations that hold the entire operation steady.

The Reflection

What details did you quietly skip today? Which ones did you handle well? Think about one moment where a small detail created unnecessary rework, tension, or confusion. What signal did that moment send about your preparation or discipline? Now think of a detail you managed cleanly—what confidence did it create?

Attention to detail is not pressure; it is posture. It is how you show others—and yourself—that the work matters, and that you can be trusted with more.

The Commitment

- I will handle the small details before they grow into disruptions.
- I will treat details as signals of my credibility, not optional extras.
- I will slow down just enough to verify the things that matter.
- I will build a reputation for work that doesn't need to be rechecked.

EBR Principle

Details reveal discipline; the small things you honor become the reputation you earn.

Day 14 — The Difference Between Motion And Progress

The Lesson

Motion is seductive. It feels like movement, like effort, like momentum. It creates the sensation of productivity without requiring the discipline of actual results. Progress, on the other hand, is quieter. It doesn't always feel fast. It doesn't always look busy. But progress is directional—motion is not. And if you don't learn to separate the two, your days will fill with activity that never advances the mission.

Motion is checking boxes. Progress is moving the outcome.
Motion is staying busy. Progress is staying aligned.
Motion burns energy. Progress conserves it.
Motion makes you tired. Progress makes you effective.

Sustainable performers understand this difference instinctively. They don't confuse effort with impact. They don't measure their day by how much they touched, but by how much they moved. This requires honesty—the kind of honesty that forces you to confront whether your busyness is creating results or simply helping you avoid the real work.

The danger is that motion looks responsible. It looks disciplined. It looks productive. But motion without direction creates drift. It burns your best cognitive hours on low-impact activities. It gives you the illusion of progress while the mission stands still. And once you're in motion, it's easy to stay in motion—because it feels safer than making the decisions that true progress demands.

Progress, in contrast, requires prioritization. It requires clarity. It requires the courage to stop working on things that don't matter, even if they feel urgent. Sustainable performance lives in that honesty. When you choose progress over motion, your work becomes leaner, your focus becomes sharper, and your time begins to generate actual results.

The Reflection

Where did you confuse motion for progress today? Think of one moment when you stayed busy but didn't move the outcome. What pulled you toward activity instead of impact? Was it avoidance, uncertainty, habit, or simply momentum?

Now consider where you made real progress—what did that feel like? What was different about your clarity, your confidence, your posture? Progress leaves a different imprint on the mind; learn to recognize it and pursue it deliberately.

The Commitment

- I will measure my day by outcomes, not activity.
- I will identify the tasks that actually move the mission and focus on those first.
- I will break the habit of using busyness as proof of productivity.
- I will choose progress over motion, even when motion feels easier.

EBR Principle

Activity burns energy; aligned action builds momentum.

Day 15 — Not All Tasks Deserve Equal Cognitive Effort

The Lesson

Your mind is a finite resource. It is not a bottomless well of clarity, focus, and decision-making strength. Yet most people distribute their cognitive effort as if every task deserves the same level of attention. This is one of the fastest ways to burn out your best thinking on work that doesn't deserve it—and one of the primary reasons high performers feel exhausted without feeling effective.

Sustainable performance begins with a simple truth: **not all tasks are equal, and they should not be treated as if they are.** Some tasks require your sharpest thinking. Others require basic presence. Some require creativity. Others require muscle memory. Some directly move the mission. Others merely support it. If you don't distinguish between them, your mind will spend its best fuel on the least impactful work.

Treating every task the same creates two problems. First, you over-invest in low consequence tasks, spending precision-level energy on something that only requires routine-level attention. Second, you under-invest in high consequence work, arriving mentally depleted when the task finally demands sharp judgment or careful decision-making. This imbalance slowly erodes both quality and consistency.

Sustainable performers think like strategists, not sprinters. They calibrate their cognitive effort to the true weight of the task. They recognize that the mind is not just a tool but a battery—and batteries drain faster when used on the wrong settings. They give their clearest hours to high-value work, their steady hours to maintenance work, and their lowest-energy hours to tasks that are repetitive, simple, or mechanical.

This discipline isn't just about productivity—it's about respect. Respect for the work that matters, respect for the work that doesn't, and respect for the finite mental bandwidth that makes sustainable performance possible in the first place.

Sustainable Performance – A 30-Day Mindsets Transformation Guide

The Reflection

Where did your mind go today? Did you burn premium cognitive fuel on low-impact tasks? Did you find yourself mentally empty just as you reached your most important work? Think back to a moment where the outcome suffered because you arrived mentally tired. How much of that fatigue was caused by investing too much brainpower in something that didn't deserve it?

What would change if you saved your clarity for the tasks that actually require clarity?

The Commitment

- Today I will match my level of attention to the true importance of the task.
- I will stop overthinking low-value work and under-preparing for high-value work.
- I will protect my clearest cognitive hours for the tasks that matter most.
- I will treat my mind like a finite resource, not an unlimited engine.

EBR Principle

When you give every task equal effort, nothing gets your best; when you allocate wisely, the right work receives the clarity it deserves.

Day 16 — The Cognitive Priority Matrix (Urgent Vs Important)

The Lesson

Long before it became a productivity framework, the distinction between urgency and importance was a leadership principle taught—and lived—by President Dwight D. Eisenhower. As both a five-star general and a U.S. president, Eisenhower understood something most people never learn: the world will constantly hand you urgent things, but only you can identify the important ones.

From that mindset came the model we now call the **Eisenhower Matrix**, the backbone of modern prioritization. It is elegant, simple, and brutally honest:

- **Urgent + Important** — Act now. These tasks shape the mission and carry real consequence.
- **Not Urgent + Important** — Schedule it. This is where strategy, planning, and progress live.
- **Urgent + Not Important** — Delegate it. Urgency does not equal value.
- **Not Urgent + Not Important** — Eliminate it. These are distractions disguised as options.

The brilliance of Eisenhower's thinking is that he understood human nature. Urgency screams. Importance whispers. And unless you consciously decide to listen to the whisper, the scream will dominate your day.

Most people operate reactively, living in the tension between the first and third quadrants—urgent work that matters and urgent work that doesn't. They end the day exhausted, not because they lacked effort, but because they lacked separation. Their mind chased urgency instead of directing importance.

Sustainable performers approach the matrix the way Eisenhower did: with deliberate restraint. They protect the second quadrant—important but not urgent—because they know this is where the future is built. Planning, preparation, improvement, and long-range decisions all live there. When you honor Quadrant 2, you shrink Quadrant 1 and starve Quadrant 3. Your life, your thinking, and your execution stabilize.

Eisenhower was right: your time is not determined by what demands your attention but by what deserves it.

The Reflection

Where did Eisenhower's lesson show up in your day? Did urgency win? Or did importance guide you? Think of one moment where you reacted to noise instead of directing your attention toward something meaningful. Why did urgency feel stronger?

Now name one important thing you postponed simply because it wasn't screaming. What would shift if you treated those quiet things as the true drivers of your future?

The Commitment

- I will sort tasks through Eisenhower's lens: urgent, important, both, or neither.
- I will intentionally protect time for important, non-urgent work.
- I will resist the pull of urgency when it lacks value.
- I will prioritize based on consequence, not volume.

EBR Principle

Urgency pressures you; importance guides you—choose the voice that shapes your future.

Day 17 — Cognitive Task Criticality: High vs. Standard vs. Low

The Lesson

Not every task deserves the same weight, and not every task deserves the same version of you. Cognitive Task Criticality is the discipline of deciding **how much of your mind** a task genuinely requires—before you begin. Without this calibration, you waste clarity on the wrong work and starve the right work of the attention it needs.

There are three levels of cognitive criticality:

High-Criticality Tasks
These tasks carry consequence. They shape outcomes, carry risk, involve judgment, or influence others. High-criticality work demands your sharpest cognition—clean focus, no switching, no divided attention. You should bring your best energy, your best clarity, and your best discipline. Treat these tasks casually and the cost will always show up later.

Standard-Criticality Tasks
These tasks matter, but not at the level of consequence. They require competence, not peak cognition. Standard-criticality work is the backbone of your day—emails, updates, small decisions, routine problem-solving. Done well, they keep your system healthy; over-invested in, they drain your mental battery for no good reason.

Low-Criticality Tasks
These tasks have almost no mental consequence. They are administrative, mechanical, routine, or autopilot in nature. They require presence, not precision. Treating these tasks with high-criticality energy is a fast path to burnout because you pour premium fuel into a low-octane engine.

Sustainable performers separate these levels instantly. They don't approach a simple task with the same intensity they give to a mission-critical decision. They know which tasks deserve peak hours and which ones can ride the edges of the day. They don't confuse impact with activity or consequence with convenience.

The purpose of Cognitive Task Criticality is simple:
Save your sharpest mind for the work that demands a sharp mind.

Everything else gets the version of you that matches its true weight—no more, no less.

The Reflection

Where did you misallocate your mind today? Did you bring high-level energy to a low-level task? Or did you arrive mentally drained to something that required your best thinking? Think of one moment where the outcome suffered because your mind wasn't matched to the task's true criticality. What would change if you pre-labeled the tasks in your day as high, standard, or low before you ever started?

Clarity is not just choosing what to do—it's choosing *how much of yourself* each task deserves.

The Commitment

- I will label tasks by criticality before beginning them.
- I will give high-criticality tasks my clearest cognitive hours.
- I will stop over-investing premium energy on low-criticality work.
- I will protect my mind from misallocation by matching effort to consequence.

EBR Principle

Your best thinking is limited—spend it where the consequences are highest.

Day 18 — The One-Decision Rule: Make Once, Apply Many

The Lesson

Most of the exhaustion people feel during the day doesn't come from the work—it comes from the number of decisions they have to make about the work. The mind drains quickly when it must repeatedly re-decide, re-confirm, or re-think something that should have been settled long ago. Sustainable performers eliminate this waste with a simple discipline called **The One-Decision Rule:**

> **Make the right decision once, then let that decision carry you forward again and again.**

This is not laziness; it's design. And it is deeply aligned with the spirit of Evidence-Based Reliability.

EBR is built on systems, not emotional reactivity. It favors clarity over improvisation, structure over whim, and deliberate standards over continual renegotiation. The One-Decision Rule embodies all three. When you establish a standard—how you prepare, how you prioritize, how you communicate, how you respond to drift—you remove the need to continually burn cognitive energy making the same decision in slightly different forms.

This is why the One-Decision Rule is so powerful:
- It **reduces cognitive load** by eliminating redundant decision-making.
- It **standardizes behavior**, reducing variation and inconsistency.
- It **creates repeatability**, which is the heartbeat of reliable execution.
- It **prevents drift**, because the decision is codified, not reinvented.

EBR teaches that systems create consistency, and consistency creates reliability. The One-Decision Rule is a personal version of that philosophy. You define the rule once—based on evidence, experience, or principle—and then you stop

Sustainable Performance – A 30-Day Mindsets Transformation Guide

debating with yourself. You apply the decision across every similar scenario without hesitation.

This frees your mind for the work that **actually requires** judgment. It protects your cognitive bandwidth for high-consequence thinking. And it creates a rhythm of execution where your best clarity is preserved for the moments that deserve it.

The One-Decision Rule doesn't restrict you; it liberates you from unnecessary mental friction. Once the rule is set, your mind stops negotiating and starts executing.

The Reflection

Where did you re-decide something today that should already be settled? Did you debate whether to start, when to start, how to start, or whether you really wanted to do something you've already committed to? How much energy did that silent negotiation steal?

Think of one area—your morning routine, your daily priority, your planning method, your communication style—where you could remove drag by making **one good decision** and using it as a standard instead of a debate.

The Commitment

- Today I will identify one recurring decision and turn it into a personal standard.
- I will stop renegotiating commitments that should already be settled.
- I will preserve my mental energy by reducing repetitive decision-making.
- I will apply the One-Decision Rule as a personal version of EBR discipline.

EBR Principle

Decide once with clarity, then execute with consistency—systems reduce the decisions your mind never needed to remake.

Day 19 — Familiarity Is the Slowest Teacher

The Lesson

Familiarity feels like progress, but it is one of the slowest and most unreliable teachers you can depend on. When you encounter a task repeatedly, your brain begins to piece things together: the sequence becomes more recognizable, the friction feels lower, and your confidence begins to rise. But this type of learning is passive. It depends entirely on how often the world chooses to hand you the same situation. If the reps don't come, or if they come too far apart, your competence stalls. You end up waiting for growth instead of driving it.

Many people misunderstand this and think they're "learning through experience," when in reality they're simply accumulating exposure. The problem is that exposure alone teaches reactively and unevenly. You only improve after you've already made the mistake or already paid the cost of trial-and-error. Familiarity teaches slowly because it teaches late. It does not prepare you before the moment—it corrects you after the moment. And this delay creates wide inconsistency in performance. Some days you feel sharp, other days you feel lost, all depending on whether the task has shown up recently enough to refresh the pattern.

The danger of relying on familiarity is that it gives the illusion of learning while keeping you trapped in a long learning curve. Familiarity is not a strategy; it's an accident. It asks you to trust timing, trust exposure, and trust that repetition will eventually arrive. Sustainable performance can't be built on that kind of chance. Growth that depends on opportunity is slower, costlier, and far more fragile than it needs to be. The performer who waits for familiarity improves eventually. The performer who prepares intentionally improves immediately.

The Reflection

Think back to a skill you learned mostly through trial-and-error. How many cycles did it take before your confidence felt legitimate? How much of that time was spent correcting preventable mistakes, and how much energy was wasted simply waiting for the next chance to try again?

Now consider your current responsibilities. Where are you relying on repetition to teach you? And what would your performance look like if you stopped waiting for familiar patterns and began preparing for them instead?

The Commitment

- I will stop expecting repetition to teach me what preparation should.
- I will notice where I'm relying on exposure instead of building understanding.
- I will reject accidental competence as a strategy for performance.
- I will look honestly at where familiarity has slowed my growth.

EBR Principle

Familiarity is accidental competence—earned slowly, unevenly, and at the cost of preventable mistakes.

Day 20 — Front-Loaded Learning Before the First Rep

The Lesson

Front-loaded learning is the discipline of preparing before performance, not after it. It is how elite performers shorten the learning curve, reduce early-stage mistakes, and enter tasks with the kind of fluency most people don't reach until much later. Instead of waiting for repetition to reveal the pattern, you study the pattern first. You preview the steps, visualize the sequence, rehearse the transitions, and identify the decision points before you encounter them. You are no longer stepping into the unknown; you are stepping into something you've already walked through mentally.

The power of front-loaded learning lies in its ability to eliminate cold starts. When you begin a task without preparation, your attention is consumed by figuring out the environment, interpreting the cues, and piecing together the structure. That cognitive load slows execution and introduces unnecessary error. But when you've studied first, the environment feels familiar even if it isn't. Your mind has placeholders ready. Your expectations are shaped. Your decisions are pre-wired. You're not improvising—you're navigating a map you built in advance.

Front-loaded learning shifts the role of experience. The reps no longer create the understanding; the reps reinforce the understanding. This accelerates growth dramatically. You burn fewer cycles, recover from mistakes faster, and build confidence earlier because your first attempts are informed attempts—not blind attempts. Most people wait for clarity to appear after several repetitions. Systems thinkers build clarity before the first one. Sustainable performance grows at the speed of your preparation, not at the speed of your exposure.

The Reflection

Where in your life do you experience unnecessary friction simply because you begin tasks cold? Think about the moments where your first few minutes are spent just trying to understand what's happening, who's involved, or what the expectations even are. How many times have you stepped into a meeting, opened a document, or started a task only to realize you're already behind because you're still mentally orienting yourself? That friction isn't a sign of incompetence—it's a sign of unprepared entry. And it is completely avoidable.

What would change if you replaced first-time confusion with preloaded clarity? Picture yourself walking into a conversation already knowing the landscape, anticipating the questions, and understanding the rhythm of how the issue will unfold. Imagine beginning the project with a mental outline of the steps, risks, and checkpoints already in place. Consider how different your confidence would feel if your first interaction with a situation wasn't truly your first—but the second or third time you'd walked through it in your mind.

Now go one layer deeper: How much stress would disappear if your brain didn't have to "catch up" every time you began something important?

The Commitment

- I will study tasks before I perform them.
- I will use previews, rehearsals, and mental walk-throughs as part of my execution system.
- I will no longer confuse repetition with readiness.
- I will move understanding ahead of action.
- I will enter tasks warm, not cold.

EBR Principle

Performance accelerates when understanding happens before action, not after it.

Day 21 — Rehearsal Makes Performance Feel Familiar

The Lesson

Rehearsal is the physical expression of front-loaded learning. It is the practice of stepping through a task before the moment demands it, giving your mind and body a head start that most people never take. When you rehearse—even briefly—you lower the cognitive load of the real event. Your decisions become cleaner, your timing sharper, your transitions smoother. You're not improvising your way through uncertainty; you're confirming what you've already walked through. Rehearsal builds a sense of familiarity before real familiarity exists.

Most people only rehearse under pressure: right before the presentation, right before the conversation, right before the critical moment. But true rehearsal happens much earlier, when the stakes are low, the environment is calm, and the mind is free to see the task clearly. Even a five-minute walk-through can shift your entire performance trajectory. By previewing the sequence, you install a mental script. By talking through your steps aloud, you expose assumptions. By running a dry run, you find friction points that would have become mistakes. Rehearsal is not theatrics—it is architecture.

What rehearsal really does is bridge the gap between intention and execution. Knowing what to do and doing it reliably are different skills. Rehearsal binds them. It's the difference between "I understand it conceptually" and "I can execute it when it counts." And it works across every domain: from leadership conversations to complex tasks, from physical actions to strategic decisions. Rehearsal is the mechanism that transforms preparation into confidence. When you rehearse, the moment never feels brand new—you've already been there. You begin the task with a level of familiarity that most people don't earn until their third or fourth attempt. And that changes everything about your performance.

The Reflection

Think about the moments when you felt most off-balance—not because the task was impossible, but because the opening minutes were spent trying to find your footing. How much of that instability came from stepping into the moment cold? How different would those situations have felt if you had rehearsed even a small part of the sequence beforehand? Consider how much of your stress, hesitation, or uneven execution comes not from complexity but from unfamiliarity. Rehearsal removes that unfamiliarity before it ever becomes a problem.

Now imagine applying rehearsal to the areas of your life where precision matters most. What conversations would go better if you practiced them aloud? What projects would feel lighter if you previewed the workflow before starting? What decisions would feel clearer if you rehearsed the decision points, the language, or the order of operations? Rehearsal doesn't require perfection—it requires attention. It requires stepping through the task long enough for your brain to build anchors. Your confidence grows because your mind recognizes the terrain. And once you've rehearsed, the real moment stops being a test and becomes simply the next repetition of something you've already done.

The Commitment

- I will rehearse key tasks before stepping into them.
- I will use walk-throughs and mental visualization as standard preparation tools.
- I will stop waiting for repetition to create familiarity and will create that familiarity intentionally.
- I will use rehearsal to turn uncertainty into momentum.

EBR Principle

Rehearsal turns the unfamiliar into the inevitable.

Day 22 — A System Is Strongest Without Decision Fatigue

The Lesson

One of the most overlooked barriers to sustainable performance is decision fatigue. Every choice—big or small—withdraws energy from the same mental account. By midday, most people are running on cognitive fumes not because their work is overwhelming, but because their environment forces them to decide constantly: *What should I do first? What should I wear? Where is that file? What tool do I need? What's the next step?* None of these decisions are difficult individually, but collectively they drain your capacity to think clearly and act decisively when it matters.

A strong system removes these unnecessary choices by creating structure ahead of time. When your tools have a place, you don't waste decision-making energy figuring out where they should go. When your workflow has a sequence, you don't burn mental calories deciding what to do next. When your priorities are already defined, you don't negotiate with yourself every morning. Systems reduce fatigue by reducing the number of discretionary decisions you need to make. They build a protected channel for your attention, so your energy is spent executing—not choosing.

This isn't about rigidity or control; it's about conservation. The more predictable your environment, the more cognitive bandwidth you save for the moments that truly require judgment. When your day is built on defaults, templates, checklists, and pre-structured routines, you free your mind from the noise of constant micro-choices. Decision fatigue doesn't show up all at once—it erodes your clarity quietly. But a well-designed system shields you from that erosion. It makes consistency easier because the path is already laid out. The fewer choices you must make, the more strength you have to make the *right* choices when they matter most.

The Reflection

Consider how many decisions you make before the real work of the day even begins. Think about the small choices you negotiate with yourself: what to start with, how to set up, where to look for something, how to sequence your steps. None of these decisions feel heavy in isolation, yet together they create a steady drain on your mental resources. How often do you end the day feeling exhausted, not because of the weight of the work, but because of the sheer volume of choices required to navigate it?

Now imagine an environment where most of those decisions are already made for you—not by someone else, but by your own design. What would your performance look like if the first hour of your day was frictionless? If your tools were always where they should be? If your workflow started the moment you arrived, instead of after several mental detours? Systems don't eliminate freedom; they eliminate friction. They give your brain the gift of clarity by taking unnecessary choices off your plate. Where could you build more structure so your energy is saved for the decisions that truly matter?

The Commitment

- I will eliminate unnecessary decisions by building stronger defaults.
- I will design my day so energy is spent executing, not choosing.
- I will create patterns and templates that support clarity and reduce fatigue.
- I will protect my decision-making capacity for what matters most.

EBR Principle

A good system makes the right choice the easiest choice.

Day 23 — Reduce Friction, Increase Completion

The Lesson

Execution rarely fails because people lack discipline. It fails because the starting point is too heavy. Every task carries an invisible "activation cost"—the mental effort required to begin. When that cost is high, even simple tasks feel complicated. You hesitate. You delay. You mentally negotiate. Not because the work is hard, but because the *start* is hard. Friction isn't a moral failure; it's an environmental tax. And the more friction you carry, the more discipline you think you need.

Reducing friction is one of the most powerful performance multipliers you can build into your system. When you make the starting line easy, everything downstream becomes easier. Pre-staged materials, clean workspaces, preloaded templates, organized folders, visible tools, and ready-to-go checklists all reduce activation energy. You remove the micro-barriers that slow execution before it even begins. And once the start is effortless, momentum takes over. You're no longer pushing a stalled engine—you're stepping into motion that's already been created by your environment.

The truth is that friction is not something you overcome with willpower; it's something you eliminate through design. High performers don't have more self-control—they have less friction. They prepare their environment so starting requires almost no thought. They engineer their surroundings to make action the default rather than the exception. This is the turning point in sustainable performance: recognizing that discipline is not a personality trait, but a byproduct of a well-designed environment. When friction falls, completion rises. And the ability to follow through stops being a daily battle and becomes a predictable rhythm.

The Reflection

Think about the tasks you consistently procrastinate on. Do they actually intimidate you, or is it the *start* that feels overwhelming? How much time have you lost circling the runway—gathering supplies, looking for files, deciding where to begin—before you ever take off? Friction shows up in small forms: a messy workspace, a missing tool, a confusing folder structure, a document you can't find, or steps that aren't clearly defined. Each piece may seem minor, but together they slow your progress and drain your motivation.

Now imagine removing those barriers before the task even reaches your desk. Picture walking into a room where everything you need is already in place. Imagine opening a project file that has the checklist ready, the template loaded, the next step clearly visible. How much more frequently would you start? How much more consistently would you finish? Reducing friction doesn't make tasks smaller—it makes them more approachable. Once you eliminate the things that make starting difficult, the entire arc of execution becomes lighter, faster, and more repeatable.

The Commitment

- I will design my environment to reduce friction at the starting point.
- I will pre-stage tools, materials, and information for the tasks that matter most.
- I will eliminate micro-barriers that slow me down or cause hesitation.
- I will treat friction as a design problem, not a discipline problem.

EBR Principle

Lower friction, higher follow-through.

Day 24 — Build the Environment That Matches the Identity

The Lesson

Your environment is not neutral. It is always shaping your behavior, nudging your choices, influencing your energy, and reinforcing your habits. Even when you think you're rising above it, you're being guided by it. People often try to change their performance without changing the environment that produces their performance. They change their goals, expectations, and intentions—but then return to the same cluttered workspace, the same disorganized tools, the same scattered documents, and the same inconsistent routines. They expect discipline to thrive in conditions that quietly pull them backward.

Identity-driven environments flip this script. Instead of fitting yourself into whatever surroundings you happen to have, you build surroundings that amplify who you intend to be. If you see yourself as someone who prepares early, your environment reflects that: tools staged, documents organized, systems visible. If you see yourself as someone who executes with clarity, you remove noise, clutter, and chaos. When your environment aligns with your identity, action becomes natural. You're not fighting the world around you; the world around you is supporting the person you're becoming.

This is the deeper truth of sustainable performance: your environment is the silent partner in every decision you make. It either reinforces your discipline or erodes it. The more aligned your surroundings are with your intended identity, the less energy you waste battling friction, disorder, or ambiguity. High performers don't just "work hard"—they engineer spaces that make excellence easier than sloppiness. They treat the environment as part of the system, not the backdrop. When you build an environment that matches your identity, your behavior begins to shift automatically. You don't have to push yourself into the right patterns; you simply follow the path your environment has prepared for you.

The Reflection

Think about the spaces where you spend most of your time—your desk, your workshop, your office, your digital files, your calendar. Do these environments reflect the person you *want to be*, or do they reflect old versions of you? How much of your daily friction comes from navigating spaces that are out of alignment with your intentions? Consider how often you've had the discipline but lacked the environment that made that discipline sustainable. A cluttered space creates mental drag. A disorganized system creates hesitation. A noisy environment creates decision fatigue. These small misalignments accumulate into frustration and inconsistency.

Now imagine walking into a space designed for the identity you are choosing to strengthen. Imagine a desk organized for clarity, tools laid out for efficiency, files structured for speed, and routines visible at a glance. How much easier would your work feel if your environment carried some of the load for you? When the space reflects the identity, the behavior follows naturally—not out of motivation, but out of alignment. Ask yourself: What environment would a person like me build if I fully believed in the identity I'm trying to step into?

The Commitment

- I will shape my environment to reinforce the identity I am building.
- I will eliminate surroundings that pull me toward old habits or old patterns.
- I will structure my physical and digital spaces for clarity, speed, and predictability.
- I will treat my environment as part of my execution system, not an afterthought.

EBR Principle

Identity leads; environment follows—and then environment leads you back.

Day 25 — Cadence Beats Intensity

The Lesson

Intensity is exciting, but it isn't sustainable. Anyone can perform at a high level for a day or a week when motivation spikes, deadlines loom, or adrenaline is high. But sustainable performance is built on cadence—a steady, repeatable rhythm that outlasts emotion, energy, or circumstance. Cadence gives structure to progress. It turns effort into pattern, pattern into habit, and habit into inevitability. Intensity can launch you forward, but cadence keeps you moving long after the launch energy fades.

The reason cadence outperforms intensity is simple: the human mind and body are designed for rhythms, not bursts. When you operate in occasional surges, your system never stabilizes. You oscillate between sprints and stalls—periods of massive effort followed by fatigue, avoidance, or inconsistency. Cadence removes these extremes. You set a pace you can maintain. You create checkpoints that repeat. You build a cycle that becomes predictable. This predictability is what makes execution feel less like a struggle and more like a flow state. You're not fighting to get started—your rhythm carries you.

Cadence also reduces the emotional volatility that often sabotages performance. When your success depends on feeling energized or inspired, you hand your execution over to chance. But cadence protects you from the ups and downs of mood, motivation, and timing. It becomes the metronome of your work. You show up regardless of how you feel because the rhythm itself is doing part of the work for you. Sustainable performance is never about how hard you can go in a single moment; it's about how reliably you can return to the same beat. In the long run, cadence wins every time.

The Reflection

Think about the goals or responsibilities in your life where you tend to work in waves—periods of intense focus followed by long gaps of avoidance or drift. How much energy is spent simply trying to restart what you abandoned during the stall? How much frustration comes from losing momentum and having to rebuild it over and over? These cycles are exhausting, not because the work itself is overwhelming, but because the lack of rhythm forces you to re-engage from zero every time.

Now imagine shifting from bursts to beats. Picture what would happen if the tasks that matter most in your life had a predictable cadence—daily, weekly, or monthly—where the work arrives like clockwork. No negotiating, no debating, no starting from scratch. What stress would disappear if you trusted the rhythm to guide your next action? What progress could you accumulate if your pace was consistent instead of sporadic? Cadence doesn't require perfection. It requires return. And return is where momentum is built. Ask yourself: What rhythm, once established, would make my execution feel lighter, faster, and more reliable?

The Commitment

- I will replace bursts of intensity with a cadence I can maintain.
- I will set rhythms for the tasks that matter most and honor them consistently.
- I will treat cadence as a system, not a preference.
- I will trust the beat more than the mood.

EBR Principle

Intensity starts the race; cadence finishes it.

Day 26 — Small Cycles Are the Engine of Big Wins

The Lesson

Big goals collapse under their own weight when you try to tackle them in giant, dramatic leaps. What feels inspiring at the beginning becomes overwhelming in the middle and impossible near the end. Sustainable performance solves this by breaking ambition into small, repeatable cycles—tight loops of action, review, and adjustment that build progress without burning you out. Small cycles don't look impressive from the outside, but they are the structural backbone of every long-term success story. They keep momentum alive when motivation fades and maintain direction when complexity rises.

Here is the truth most performers overlook: "Small goals create small victories. Small victories create the confidence for larger goals." This is not just a motivational slogan—it's a structural principle. When you break work into small cycles, you create winnable moments. Those wins reinforce belief. That belief strengthens identity. That identity fuels larger ambitions. It is the psychology of progress working hand in hand with the architecture of execution. Each small cycle becomes a confidence deposit, making the next level of difficulty feel possible—and eventually inevitable.

The brilliance of small cycles is that they reduce risk while increasing clarity. Instead of betting everything on a massive plan that only reveals its flaws too late, you learn in small increments. You move, you examine, you adjust. Each cycle refines your understanding. Each loop sharpens your execution. This protects you from the runaway error—the mistake that compounds for months because it wasn't caught early enough. Small cycles prevent drift. They keep you aligned, calibrated, and paying attention to what actually works rather than what you hope will work. In the long arc, big wins are never the result of big efforts—they're the result of small cycles executed faithfully.

The Reflection

Think about the areas of your life where progress feels stalled. Are you trying to take steps that are too big, too infrequent, or too dependent on bursts of energy? Consider how often you've created grand plans that fell apart because they lacked a sustainable rhythm. Without small cycles, everything becomes heavier: decisions take longer, frustration builds faster, and setbacks feel personal instead of procedural. You're not failing because you lack ability—you're failing because the structure is too large to sustain.

Now imagine shrinking the scale. Imagine breaking your work into cycles so small they feel easy to start and easy to repeat. Picture what would happen if every few days—or every day—you took one deliberate step, reviewed the result, and adjusted the next step accordingly. How much momentum could you build? How much clarity could you gain? Small cycles might not feel dramatic, but they create the conditions where consistency thrives. Ask yourself: What important goal could become achievable if I stopped working in giant pushes and started working in small, dependable loops?

The Commitment

- I will break big goals into small, repeatable cycles.
- I will value consistent loops over dramatic leaps.
- I will use review-and-adjust rhythms to stay aligned and reduce drift.
- I will build momentum through tiny, deliberate steps.

EBR Principle

Small cycles move mountains—one predictable loop at a time.

Day 27 — Execution Strengthens Through Feedback, Not Memory

The Lesson

Most people assume their execution will improve automatically with time—that if they simply do a task often enough, their memory will store the lessons and their performance will gradually refine. But memory is a weak, inconsistent teacher. It forgets details, blurs context, and simplifies complexity. It remembers the emotional parts and loses the procedural ones. Sustainable performance does not grow through memory; it grows through feedback—through the deliberate act of reviewing what happened, identifying why it happened, and adjusting what should happen next.

Feedback is powerful because it closes the loop between intention and reality. Without feedback, you repeat the same mistakes, sometimes for years, believing that experience alone will eventually fix them. But experience without reflection is just repetition. You're doing more, but you're not becoming better. Feedback changes that. It forces clarity. It reveals blind spots. It exposes assumptions. It separates what you think you did from what you actually did. And once you see the gap clearly, improvement becomes inevitable rather than accidental.

The strength of feedback is that it accelerates growth by shortening the learning cycle. Instead of waiting for memory to eventually piece together what went wrong, you analyze immediately. You capture insights while they're fresh. You adjust before the next cycle begins. This builds a learning rhythm that compounds over time. The performer who uses feedback improves faster than the performer who relies on memory—because feedback is intentional while memory is unpredictable. Sustainable performance is not about doing more; it's about learning faster. And feedback is the engine of that acceleration.

The Reflection

Think about the tasks or responsibilities where you've struggled to improve, even though you've done them many times. Are you truly learning from those repetitions, or are you just repeating them and hoping they'll eventually get easier? Consider how often you've trusted your memory to retain the specifics of what went wrong, only to find yourself making the same mistake again weeks later. Memory is slippery. It loses nuance. It bends the story to protect your ego or justify your action. Without feedback, your understanding stays shallow, and your improvement stays slow.

Now imagine applying a structured feedback loop to the areas that matter most: a short review after a meeting, a quick note after completing a project step, a brief reflection after a conversation or decision. Picture how much clarity you could gain if every cycle ended with insight rather than assumption. Feedback reduces confusion. It replaces guesswork with evidence. It turns every repetition into a learning moment. Ask yourself: What part of my execution would transform the fastest if I stopped trusting my memory and started trusting my feedback?

The Commitment

- I will rely on feedback more than memory to guide my improvement.
- I will review key actions and decisions to capture lessons while they're fresh.
- I will use evidence, not assumption, to refine my performance.
- I will treat feedback as a requirement, not an optional step.

EBR Principle

Feedback sharpens what memory blurs.

Day 28 — Failure Is Not a Detour; It's the Data Stream

The Lesson

Most people experience failure as a verdict—a statement about their talent, their potential, or their worth. But in the world of sustainable performance, failure isn't a verdict at all. It's data. It's how the system speaks to you. Every mistake, every misstep, every unexpected outcome carries the information you need to refine the next cycle. When you remove the ego from failure, what's left is an incredibly powerful feedback stream. Failure loses its sting because the story around it disappears, leaving behind only the signal.

The fundamental difference between high performers and everyone else is not that high performers fail less—it's that they *extract more from the failure*. They treat it like an input, not an insult. They don't internalize the mistake; they analyze it. They don't run from discomfort; they study it. They don't overreact to variance; they interrogate it. Failure becomes part of their execution architecture, not a disruption to it. Sustainable performance demands this posture, because no system—no matter how well designed—will unfold perfectly. The learning comes from the deviation.

When you embrace failure as data, you stop fearing the moment something goes wrong. Your emotional posture changes. You become calmer, more curious, more analytical. Instead of panicking, you ask: *What is this moment trying to show me? What structural weakness did this expose? What small adjustment will prevent this next time?* Failure becomes a teacher, not a threat. And over time, the performer who mines failure for insight outpaces the performer who spends energy trying to avoid it. Failure doesn't slow you down—it accelerates you, if you treat it as information rather than identity.

The Reflection

Think about a recent failure that weighed heavily on you. How much of the weight came from the actual consequences—and how much came from the meaning you attached to it? So often, what hurts is not the event but the story we tell ourselves about the event: *I should have known better. I shouldn't have made that mistake. This proves I'm behind. This proves I'm not good enough.* None of these interpretations are data. They are emotional narratives masquerading as insight.

Now imagine stripping the story away and looking at the failure with clean eyes. What did it reveal about your preparation, your assumptions, your rhythm, or your system? What friction point did it expose? What blind spot did it highlight? What small correction could you make that would prevent the same outcome next time? Failure becomes lighter the moment you turn it into information. And once you treat it as the data stream of improvement, execution becomes less about avoiding mistakes—and more about learning from them faster than anyone else.

The Commitment

- I will treat failure as data, not identity.
- I will extract insight from mistakes instead of attaching emotion to them.
- I will use failure to refine my systems, rhythms, and assumptions.
- I will respond to deviation with analysis rather than self-judgment.

EBR Principle

Failure isn't a setback—it's the signal.

Day 29 — Create Confidence Through Transferable Performance

The Lesson

Most people think confidence comes from talent or personality. They assume confident performers are simply built differently—more self-assured, more gifted, more naturally composed. But real confidence does not come from talent; it comes from *transferability*. It comes from having systems that travel with you from situation to situation. When you have a way of thinking, a way of preparing, a way of breaking down tasks, and a way of executing that works everywhere—you stop fearing new environments, new challenges, and new expectations. You recognize the landscape may change, but *you don't*.

A system is confidence you can carry. It gives you a method for choosing priorities, structuring your workflow, reducing friction, rehearsing actions, and learning from feedback—no matter where you are or what you're facing. This means your performance no longer depends on whether you've seen the situation before. You have something better than familiarity—you have architecture. You have a process that produces consistent behavior, even when the conditions vary. And this stability is what confidence feels like: not bravado, not positive thinking, but the deep certainty that your approach is sound.

A person without a system must rely on memory, adrenaline, or luck. Their confidence rises and falls with circumstances. But a person with a system enters situations already grounded. They don't need to know everything—they only need to know how to run their method. This is why high performers appear calm in unfamiliar territory: they are not calm because the situation is easy; they are calm because they brought their system with them. Sustainable performance is built on this kind of transferable confidence—the kind that isn't shaken by new problems because it never depended on comfort in the first place.

The Reflection

Think about moments when your confidence fell apart—not because you lacked skill, but because you felt unprepared or unsure how to approach the situation. How much of that anxiety came from not having a structure to lean on? Consider how often your confidence fluctuates based on familiarity: you feel strong when you've seen the problem before and uncertain when you haven't. That's not a talent issue—it's a system issue. Without a transferable process, every new challenge feels like starting from scratch.

Now imagine stepping into unfamiliar situations with the same confidence you have in familiar ones. Imagine knowing that even if the context is new, your process is not. You know how to prepare, how to organize, how to clarify, how to rehearse, how to reduce friction, how to cycle, how to learn. What would your leadership look like if confidence came not from comfort, but from method? What opportunities would you pursue if you trusted your system more than your circumstances?

The Commitment

- I will build systems I can carry into any environment.
- I will pursue confidence through structure, not emotion.
- I will rely on method when the situation is unfamiliar.
- I will let my system, not the setting, determine my level of certainty.

EBR Principle

Confidence travels when systems travel.

Sustainable Performance – A 30-Day Mindsets Transformation Guide

Day 30 — The Architecture Becomes the Identity

The Lesson

At the beginning of this journey, execution may have felt like something you *did*—a set of habits, tools, and strategies you were trying to install into an already busy life. But by Day 30, something deeper has happened: the system is no longer something you reach for. It's something you *are becoming*. The architecture of sustainable performance has started to merge with your identity. The behaviors you once had to remember now feel natural. The structures you once had to build now feel obvious. Rhythm replaces struggle. Clarity replaces hesitation. Design replaces willpower.

Identity shifts quietly, but decisively. A person who uses a system occasionally still sees themselves as someone fighting for discipline. A person who *builds and lives inside systems* begins to see themselves differently: as someone who prepares early, organizes intelligently, and executes predictably. Sustainable performance becomes part of how you move through the world. You don't rise and fall with your mood, your energy, or your motivation—you operate from an internal architecture that remains steady even when circumstances fluctuate.

This is the real victory of the past 30 days: you have internalized the idea that execution is not personality-dependent, inspiration-dependent, or environment-dependent. It is *system dependent*. And because systems can be built anywhere, refined anytime, and carried into any situation, your execution becomes portable. It becomes resilient. It becomes self-reinforcing. You now understand that high performance is not luck or temperament—it is structure multiplied by identity. You aren't simply "trying harder." You are becoming someone whose default mode is clarity, rhythm, and intentional action. The architecture has taken root inside you. And once identity shifts, behavior follows without friction.

The Reflection

Look back at the last month. What has changed in how you think, plan, prepare, and execute? Notice how much lighter execution feels when it runs on structure instead of sheer effort. Consider the moments where you caught yourself behaving differently—not because you forced a new habit, but because the system shaped the choice for you. That's identity-level transformation. That's evidence that the architecture has moved from the surface of your life into the foundation of who you are.

Now imagine carrying this identity forward into your next month, your next challenge, your next season. What becomes possible when predictability isn't a struggle but a signature? What opportunities open when you believe—deeply—that you can create clarity wherever you go? Identity doesn't change through intensity. It changes through rhythm. And your rhythm has been built. Ask yourself: Who am I becoming now that systems—not circumstances—define my performance?

The Commitment

- I will treat this system as part of my identity, not an optional tool.
- I will act from structure, not from mood or urgency.
- I will carry this architecture into every environment I enter.
- I will continue refining my rhythms so execution becomes easier over time.

EBR Principle

When the system becomes who you are, execution becomes inevitable.

BONUS DAY — Building a Culture That Sustains Execution

The Lesson

Sustainable performance does not scale through talent, intensity, or personality. It scales through culture—through an environment where clarity is normal, preparation is expected, rhythm is shared, and systems are honored. Culture is simply collective behavior repeated over time. If individuals rely on mood, motivation, or personality to perform, the team becomes unpredictable. But when individuals operate from architecture—personal systems, environmental structure, shared rhythms—the entire team becomes steady. The culture begins to carry the work.

A culture of execution forms when leaders model the behaviors they want multiplied. Leaders who plan early encourage teams that plan early. Leaders who reduce friction create teams that reduce friction. Leaders who rehearse, reflect, prepare, and operate with intentional cadence establish a standard that others instinctively follow. People do not rise to the level of organizational slogans; they rise to the level of organizational systems. When the system is clear, the culture becomes self-correcting.

This is the essence of sustainable performance at scale: the environment begins to enforce the behaviors, not the leader's personality. Processes remind people of what matters. Rhythms carry people forward when energy dips. Checklists safeguard quality. Feedback loops drive learning. Shared mental models prevent drift. Over time, execution becomes less about pushing people and more about aligning people inside a structure that makes excellence easier than sloppiness.

Culture becomes sustainable when the system becomes the default. And it becomes transformative when identity shifts—not just for the individual, but for the team. When people start saying, *"This is how we operate. This is who we are,"* execution stops being an initiative and becomes the signature of the organization. The architecture becomes the culture. The culture becomes the advantage. And the advantage compounds.

The Reflection

Consider the environments you've been part of—teams, workplaces, units, families—where execution felt predictable and strong. What made them work? Chances are it wasn't talent. It wasn't intensity. It wasn't hope. It was rhythm. It was structure. It was shared expectations and consistent behavior. Now think about the environments that were chaotic or exhausting. What was missing? Not motivation. Not intelligence. Structure. Alignment. Clear standards. Shared discipline. Culture always becomes whatever is easiest to repeat.

Now look at your team today—your family, your department, your peers, your circle, or the people who watch how you operate. What would happen if your personal systems became the standard others followed? What would shift if your preparation, your execution rhythm, your clarity, and your discipline quietly influenced the entire environment? Leadership is not loud. It is contagious. And the greatest contribution you can make to any team is to live in a way that makes execution feel natural, repeatable, and inevitable for everyone around you.

The Commitment

- I will model the behaviors I want multiplied in the environments I influence.
- I will build systems that others can see, follow, and trust.
- I will contribute to a culture where clarity, preparation, and rhythm are the norm.
- I will lead in a way that makes sustainable performance easier for everyone around me.

EBR Principle

Culture is the echo of your systems—repeated through your team.

The Sustainable Performance Checklist

1. Clarity Before Action

- Define the mission in one sentence.
- Identify the three non-negotiables for today.
- Confirm the priority sequence (Primary → Supporting → Administrative).
- Identify any unknowns that require recon.

2. Prepare the Environment

- Clear workspace — remove visual friction.
- Stage tools, documents, and reference materials.
- Pre-load templates, checklists, and files.
- Confirm the environment matches the identity you intend to operate from.

3. Run the 1/3–1/3–1/3 Rule

- **1/3 Planning:** What is the sequence? What are the decision points?
- **1/3 Gear Prep:** What must be staged, checked, or tested?
- **1/3 Rehearsal:** Mental walk-through, dry run, or verbal run-through.

4. Execute With Rhythm, Not Emotion

- Maintain cadence (daily/weekly/tempo cycles).
- Start small; reduce activation friction.
- Use micro-cycles: Act → Review → Adjust.
- Protect cognitive bandwidth by using defaults and templates.

5. Monitor Cognitive State

- Check for fatigue signals.
- Shift gears when needed.
- Manage your activation threshold — don't begin cold.

6. Use Feedback Instead of Memory

- Capture three notes immediately after key actions.
- Identify drift, friction, or unexpected outcomes.
- Apply corrections to the *next* cycle, not the current one.

7. Strengthen Identity Through Structure

- Align workspace with who you are becoming.
- Reinforce small wins to build larger confidence.
- Let systems, not mood, dictate execution.

8. Conduct Daily Stabilization

- Close loops: communications, tasks, decisions.
- Update the PACE plan as needed.
- Stage tomorrow's environment before leaving.

9. Transition Cleanly

- Document status, risks, and next actions.
- Clear mental residue through reflection and reset.
- End in order so the next day begins in order.

The Criticality & Priority Matrix

A Tool for Fast, Repeatable Prioritization

	URGENT	NOT URGENT
High Criticality	**A1 – Critical & Urgent** Immediate attention; Non-Negotiable	**A2 – Critical but NOT Urgent** High-Value, strategic focus; Schedule Proactively
Standard Criticality	**B1 – Standard & Urgent** Process quickly; Use SOP to move cleanly	**B2 – Standard & NOT Urgent** Plan & batch efficiently; Avoid unnecessary urgency
Low Criticality	**C1 – Low Value & Urgent** Triage, time-box, or redirect; Avoid emotional urgency	**C2 – Low Value & NOT Urgent** Delegate, defer, or archive; Optional, background work

HOW TO USE THE MATRIX

1. Determine Criticality First (Impact, Not Emotion)

Criticality asks:
"If this fails, what is the impact?"

- **High Criticality:** Severe impact; affects mission, safety, credibility, timelines, customers, or leadership expectations.
- **Standard Criticality:** Normal operational importance; must be done correctly but not catastrophic.
- **Low Criticality:** Minimal consequence; convenience-level tasks.

Never begin with urgency. Begin with impact.

2. Determine Urgency Second (Time Sensitivity)

Urgency asks:
"Is the required time window collapsing?"

- **Urgent:** Must move today. A deadline, dependency, or downstream blocker exists.
- **Not Urgent:** Can be scheduled without damage or loss.

Urgency without criticality is almost always noise.

ACTION GUIDELINES (For Each Category)

A1 — High Criticality + Urgent ("Do Now")

- Immediate execution.
- No delegation without full context.
- Use PACE plan to avoid single-point failures.
- Reduce distractions; go into "single-mission mode."
- Document outcomes for chain-of-command clarity.

A2 — High Criticality + Not Urgent ("Schedule With Intention")

- These are the *most important tasks in your system.*
- Block calendar time in advance.
- Use rehearsal, pre-staging, and small cycles.
- Protect these from interruption—they shape reputation.

B1 — Standard Criticality + Urgent ("Process Cleanly")

- Use SOPs and checklists to prevent rushed errors.
- Move quickly but not sloppily.
- Keep emotional urgency out of tactical execution.
- Time-box to remain efficient.

B2 — Standard Criticality + Not Urgent ("Batch & Maintain Rhythm")

- Group similar tasks into blocks.
- Perfect for daily or weekly maintenance cycles.
- Avoid allowing these to drift until they become urgent.

C1 — Low Criticality + Urgent ("Triage or Redirect")

- Question why it's urgent—real or emotional?
- Delegate when possible.
- Time-box strictly (5–10 minutes max).
- Avoid letting low-value noise hijack High-Criticality work.

C2 — Low Criticality + Not Urgent ("Defer, Delegate, or Delete")

- These tasks often add clutter, not value.
- Keep in a "parking lot" list.
- Review weekly and eliminate aggressively.
- Only act on them if they support a strategic goal.

FAST PRIORITY RULES (Memorization-Ready)

- **Impact > Urgency.**
- **Criticality before clock.**
- **Schedule A2 before processing B1.**
- **C1 gets triage; C2 gets ignored unless it climbs.**
- **If everything is urgent, nothing is prioritized.**
- **If everything is critical, your system is broken.**

USAGE NOTE

Print this and keep it:

- On your desk
- In your planning notebook
- At the top of your digital task system
- As a daily check during morning and midday resets

This matrix becomes powerful when it is used **every single day** to eliminate noise and protect your best attention.

The PACE Builder Card

Primary • Alternate • Contingency • Emergency

Use this card to build a clear, layered plan before executing any mission or task. Identify your Primary path first, then deliberately design Alternate, Contingency, and Emergency options so you never face a single point of failure. Review the triggers, transitions, and assumptions behind each layer to ensure you can pivot smoothly when conditions change.

1. Mission Statement

1. Define the mission in one clear sentence.
2. Focus on outcome, not activity.
3. Clarify what "complete" means and what "success" looks like.
4. Identify constraints, boundaries, and non-negotiables.

2. PRIMARY (P)

Your expected plan — the preferred, most efficient path.
Should be the cleanest, simplest, and most direct way to achieve the mission.

Elements of the Primary Path:

- Core method or approach
- Required tools, resources, or people
- Conditions that must be true
- Critical assumptions behind the plan
- Known friction points
- Trigger criteria that signal you must shift to the Alternate

3. ALTERNATE (A)

A fully viable backup — same mission, different route.
Should be nearly as strong as the Primary, just less optimal.

Elements of the Alternate Path:

- Different means to the same end
- Resources or tools that differ from Primary
- When and why you would select this path
- Tradeoffs (speed vs. complexity, effort vs. reliability)
- Signals that tell you the Primary is degrading

4. CONTINGENCY (C)

Used when both Primary and Alternate break down.
A less efficient but still workable way to achieve the mission.
Often requires improvisation, reduced output, or slower execution.

Elements of the Contingency Path:

- Reduced-resource option
- Workarounds and acceptable improvisations
- Minimum viable output required for success
- Environmental or situational triggers for switching
- Risks and cost of operating in this mode

5. EMERGENCY (E)

Worst-case scenario plan — protects people, assets, timelines, or credibility. This path may not complete the mission, but it prevents collapse.

Elements of the Emergency Path:

- Life-safety, reputation, or mission-protection actions
- Stop-gap measures to maintain stability
- Immediate steps to prevent further loss
- Roles and chain-of-command expectations
- Threshold triggers for activating Emergency mode

6. PACE Review Questions

Ask these before executing:

- What assumptions am I making in the Primary plan?
- What failure signals will tell me to switch early?
- Are my Alternate and Contingency options realistic?
- Does my Emergency plan protect both mission and people?
- Do all paths align with the mission intent?
- What is the quickest, safest pivot point between options?

7. PACE Best Practices

- Build the PACE before you begin — not during.
- Rehearse the transition points between P → A → C → E.
- Keep each path simple enough to run during stress.
- Share the PACE plan with your team to reduce confusion.
- Update the PACE whenever conditions change.
- Treat the Emergency option as a last-resort stabilization plan.

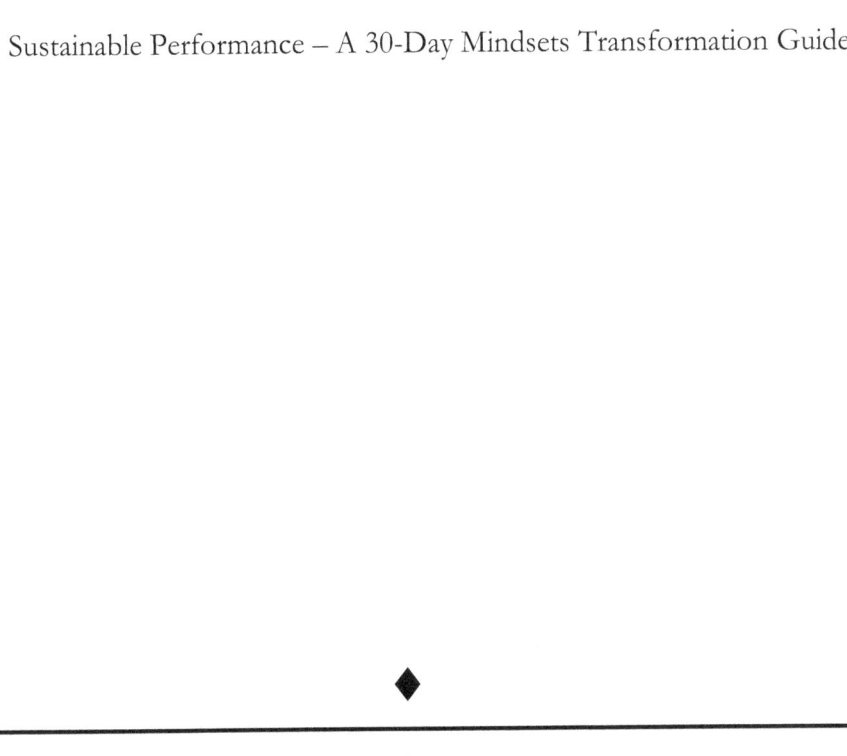

Sustainable Performance – A 30-Day Mindsets Transformation Guide

The Cognitive Gears Quick Card

The Five Cognitive Modes That Drive Sustainable performance

GEAR 1 — SCANNING (Wide Awareness)

Purpose: Gain situational understanding before acting.

Use When: Starting a task, evaluating environment, identifying risks, feeling uncertain.

Characteristics: Observing, gathering context, mapping terrain.

Warnings: Don't stay here too long — scanning without deciding creates drift.

GEAR 2 — FOCUSING (Narrowed Attention)

Purpose: Direct energy onto a single task or decision.

Use When: You know what matters and must move deliberately.

Characteristics: Reduced noise, centered attention, high intentionality.

Warnings: Over-focusing too early causes blind spots; confirm the scan first.

GEAR 3 — EXECUTING (Action Mode)

Purpose: Convert clarity into movement; follow the plan with rhythm.

Use When: Steps are identified, risks are known, environment is staged.

Characteristics: Steady tempo, predictable cycles, low hesitation.

Warnings: Avoid improvisation unless conditions change; execute what you planned.

GEAR 4 — ADAPTING (Flexibility Mode)

Purpose: Adjust to real-time changes without losing direction.
Use When: Plans degrade, new constraints appear, or the unexpected shows up.
Characteristics: Calm pivoting, pattern recognition, recomposing the "next good option."
Warnings: Don't confuse adapting with abandoning the mission — maintain intent.

GEAR 5 — ANALYZING (Reflection Mode)

Purpose: Extract insight from outcomes; identify friction, drift, or structural flaws.
Use When: Closing a loop, ending a cycle, after key actions or errors.
Characteristics: Objectivity, curiosity, data-driven learning.
Warnings: Avoid turning analysis into self-judgment; stay focused on the system.

NEUTRAL MODE — RESET (Cognitive Recovery)

Purpose: Reduce overload, clear emotional residue, and regain decision quality.
Use When: Fatigue, frustration, uncertainty, or degraded performance.
Characteristics: Breathing, stepping away, re-centering, re-grounding.
Warnings: Do not make decisions in Neutral — this is a recovery mode, not an action mode.

When to Shift Gears

Shift gears intentionally when:

- Clarity is low (shift to Scanning)
- Overwhelm or noise rises (shift to Neutral)
- Priority is known (shift to Focusing)
- Conditions are stable (shift to Executing)
- Something breaks or deviates (shift to Adapting)
- The task ends (shift to Analyzing)

Cognitive Gear Principles

- Don't execute in Scanning mode.
- Don't adapt without first anchoring to intent.
- Don't analyze while emotionally activated.
- Don't treat Neutral as avoidance — use it for recovery.
- Don't mix gears; run one at a time with intention.

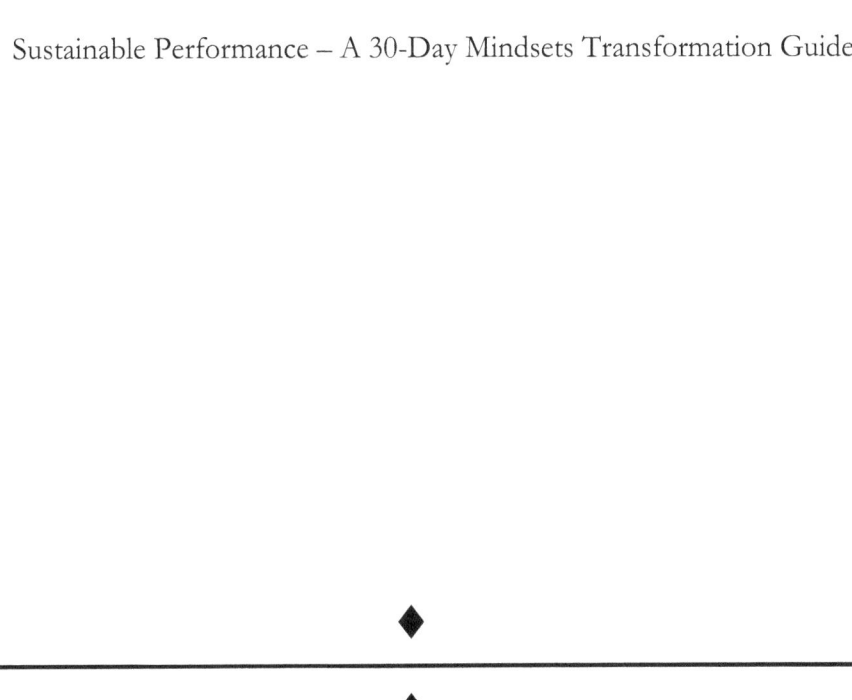

The Ten Signals of Cognitive Fatigue

A Quick Diagnostic for Recognizing Degraded Decision Quality

1. Slowed Thinking

Decisions take longer, simple choices feel heavy, and mental processing feels sluggish.

2. Shortened Attention Span

You lose focus quickly, bounce between tasks, or struggle to stay with a single thread.

3. Emotional Reactivity

Irritation, defensiveness, or frustration surface more easily — emotion begins driving logic.

4. Impulse Decisions

You choose quickly just to "get it off your plate," skipping the mental checks you normally use.

5. Avoidance Patterns

You procrastinate, delay, or mentally withdraw from tasks that would normally be manageable.

6. Inconsistent Execution

Your performance fluctuates, you miss small details, or you overlook steps you'd normally catch.

7. Increased Errors

You make small mistakes more frequently — typos, missing steps, wrong attachments, mis-clicks.

8. Reduced Working Memory

You forget what you were doing mid-task or struggle to remember instructions or next steps.

9. Decision Looping

You rethink the same decision repeatedly, unable to commit or move forward.

10. Loss of Perspective

Everything begins to feel urgent, heavy, or overwhelming — the ability to prioritize degrades.

The Drift Detection Guide

How to Spot Early Indicators of Destabilization in Your Own Execution

- Drift is what happens when you slowly slide away from your system without noticing.
- It never feels dramatic at first — it feels subtle, explainable, "temporary."
- But drift is the root cause behind most breakdowns in execution, clarity, and performance.

These signals help you detect drift early, before it compounds.

THE EIGHT EARLY WARNING SIGNS OF DRIFT

1. Rising Friction

Tasks feel heavier than normal.
You hesitate more, start slower, or keep rearranging the same work without acting.

2. Lost Rhythm

Cadence breaks down.
You skip blocks, abandon routines, or let daily/weekly cycles slip out of sync.

3. Increasing Clutter

Your workspace, digital files, or task lists start getting messy again.
Visual and mental noise return.

4. Emotional Decision-Making

You start reacting instead of responding — urgency takes over priority, feelings override clarity.

5. Deviating From Your PACE Plan

You improvise more.
You move from Primary directly into Emergency mode without using Alternate or Contingency layers.

6. Rising Rework and Repetitions

You redo tasks more often, correct avoidable mistakes, or retrace steps you normally get right the first time.

7. Reduced Preparation

You stop rehearsing, stop scanning, or stop staging.
You begin stepping into tasks "cold."

8. Weak or Missing Feedback Loops

You no longer review your performance at the end of the day.
You rely on memory instead of evidence, or you stop adjusting your system at all.

DRIFT RECOVERY PROTOCOL

When you notice drift:

1. Pause and go to Neutral Mode
Reset mentally before touching the task.

2. Re-scan the situation
What changed? What assumption broke? What friction returned?

3. Rebuild the next cycle small
Shrink the task. Reduce decision load. Re-establish cadence.

4. Re-stage the environment
Clear clutter, reload tools, reset the workspace.

5. Update your PACE plan
Where did the breakdown occur? Strengthen the Primary, refine the Alternate, rehearse the Contingency.

6. Do one clean rep
A single clean cycle re-stabilizes your system faster than pushing through chaos.

THE THREE RULES OF DRIFT DETECTION

Rule 1: Drift is subtle — if you wait until it feels serious, it's already advanced.
Rule 2: Drift is cumulative — small deviations compound into large failures.
Rule 3: Drift is reversible — the earlier you catch it, the easier the recovery.

Sustainable Performance – A 30-Day Mindsets Transformation Guide

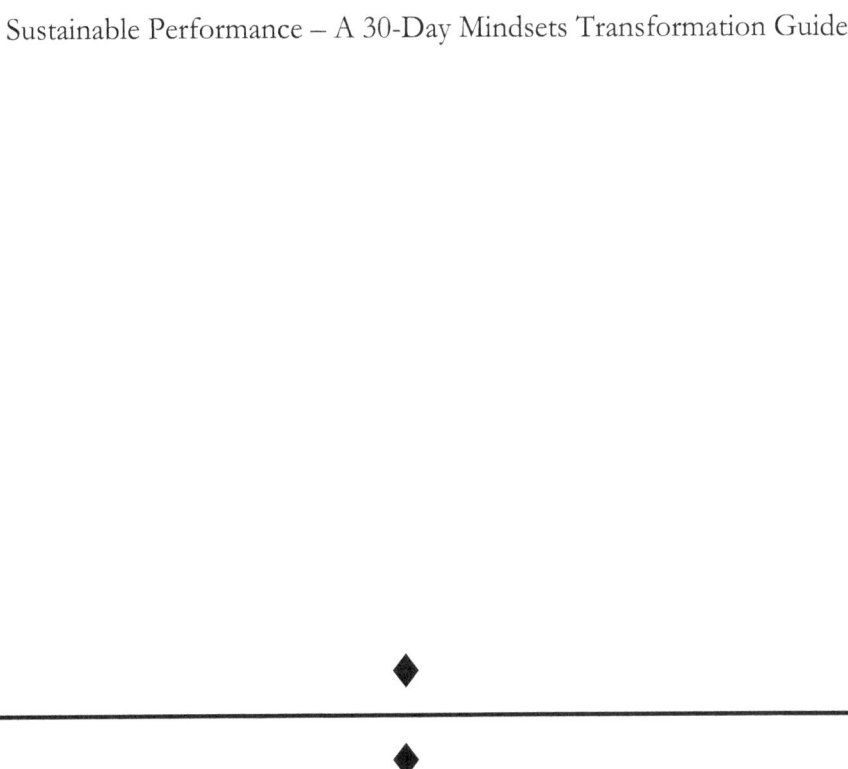

The Team Synchronization Protocol

A Simple, Repeatable Checklist for Aligning Plans, Tempo, and PACE Across the Team

Synchronized teams execute smoother, adjust faster, and make fewer mistakes. Desynchronized teams generate friction, rework, confusion, and drift.

This protocol ensures everyone begins from the same page, moves at the same tempo, and adapts using the same logic.

1. ALIGN ON THE MISSION (WHAT WE ARE DOING)

State the mission in one clear sentence.
Everyone should be able to repeat it back cleanly.
No jargon. No ambiguity. No multi-paragraph explanations.
Mission clarity eliminates 80% of team confusion.

Confirm:
- The desired outcome
- The constraints
- The non-negotiables
- The definition of "done"

2. ALIGN ON ROLES (WHO DOES WHAT)

Clarity of responsibility prevents collisions and gaps.
Confirm:
- Primary owner of each major task
- Supporting roles
- Chain-of-command for decisions
- Who to notify when conditions change
- Where authority begins and ends

Every person has a role. Every role has a boundary.

3. ALIGN ON PACE (HOW FAST WE ARE MOVING)

Teams fail when half the group is sprinting and the other half thinks it's a walk.

Confirm the day's or mission's intended tempo:
- High-tempo (rapid actions, fast turns)
- Standard-tempo (steady execution)
- Slow-tempo (careful work, detail-critical)
- Mixed-tempo (time blocks with different rhythms)

Tempo determines the cadence of communication, checkpoints, and decision timing.

4. ALIGN ON THE PACE PLAN (PRIMARY / ALTERNATE / CONTINGENCY / EMERGENCY)

Every team member must know:
- The Primary approach
- The Alternate if Primary degrades
- The Contingency if both fail
- The Emergency plan if the mission or safety is threatened

Teams fall apart when people switch paths at different times —or for different reasons.

5. ALIGN ON COMMUNICATION CHANNELS (HOW WE TALK)

Decide the channels for:
- Routine updates
- Urgent alerts
- Escalations
- Documentation
- Decision confirmations

Choose communication windows if the tempo is tight.
Clarity reduces chaos.

6. ALIGN ON CHECKPOINTS (WHEN WE RECONNECT)

Set predictable touchpoints for:
- Progress checks
- Drift detection
- Re-prioritization
- Contingency activation
- End-of-shift transitions

Short, structured syncs prevent drift and reduce the need for constant interruption.

7. ALIGN ON FAILURE SIGNALS (WHAT TRIGGERS ADAPTATION)

Define the indicators that tell the team to pivot:
- A missed dependency
- A breakdown in resources
- Conflicting priorities
- Delay that changes the timeline
- Safety or quality degradation
- New constraints

If the team shares the same triggers, adaptation becomes unified instead of fractured.

8. ALIGN ON END-OF-MISSION TRANSITION

A good team doesn't finish a mission — it transitions cleanly. Confirm:
- What must be documented
- What must be restaged
- What must be handed off
- What must be communicated upward or downward
- What needs to be reset for tomorrow

Teams that close cleanly start strong the next day.

About the Author

Andy E. Page, Jr., Ph.D.

Founder, **EBR Technologies**
Creator of the **Evidence-Based Reliability (EBR)™ and RCM-FX™** frameworks

Andy Page is a reliability engineer, strategist, and educator who has spent more than two decades helping industrial organizations transform the way they think about maintenance, performance, and culture. His work bridges two worlds — the precision of data and the discipline of leadership.

As the founder of **EBR Technologies**, Andy developed the Evidence-Based Reliability (EBR) framework, a practical approach that helps teams replace emotion with evidence and chaos with control. His **RCM-FX** method redefines classical reliability-centered maintenance with deeper categorization of failure effects, layered protection logic, and a culture-first mindset that connects the shop floor to the boardroom.

Over his career, Andy has guided clients across manufacturing, utilities, energy, and consumer goods — helping leaders and technicians alike build systems that think before they break. His teaching style combines technical clarity with cultural insight, making reliability not just a technical function, but a leadership behavior.

When he's not writing or consulting, Andy speaks to global audiences about the intersection of foresight, data, and discipline — and how evidence can become the most trusted voice in an organization.

About EBR Technologies

EBR Technologies (Evidence-Based Reliability) is a reliability consulting and training organization focused on helping clients build systems that think, plan, and act with discipline.

Founded on the belief that reliability isn't assumed — it's engineered, EBR Technologies equips organizations with tools and frameworks to:
- Engineer foresight through structured analysis and evidence-driven planning.
- Strengthen execution through Work Execution Management (WEM) systems that eliminate friction.
- **S**hape culture through the R^3/R^4 Model — aligning what leaders Require, Reward, and Reinforce with what the organization's Rituals, Rhetoric, Role Models, and Routines display.

EBR's work spans reliability improvement roadmaps, criticality analysis, PM optimization, asset walkdowns, and full-scale cultural alignment programs designed to make evidence the language of leadership.

EBR Technologies
Evidence is our authority.

www.ebrtechnologies.com
info@ebrtechnologies.com

Author's Note on the Use of AI

This book was written in collaboration with an artificial intelligence tool — not as a shortcut, but as a companion in reflection.

Every lesson, mindset, and maxim within these pages originates from my years of teaching, consulting, and field experience in safety, reliability, and culture. The principles draw from my established models — the R3/R4 Culture Framework, the Evidence-Based Thinking philosophy, and the broader discipline of Leadership Alignment that I've practiced and refined across industries and organizations.

AI served here as an instrument, not an author. Like a disciplined editor with infinite patience, it helped shape language, surface clarity, and maintain consistency across hundreds of pages. But the thoughts, logic, and voice are entirely my own. Each reflection began with lived experience — moments in real plants, real teams, and real failures that taught what alignment truly means.

The machine assisted in structure; the meaning came from the field. It allowed me to capture ideas at the speed they occurred, to test phrasing against the very principles this book teaches — precision, coherence, and intent. The goal was never to let technology think for me, but to let it think with me, mirroring the process of inquiry that defines evidence-based leadership itself.

Every page has been reviewed, edited, and approved by me to ensure it aligns with the purpose of this work. The message is unchanged, whether typed by hand or accelerated by algorithm.

This book stands as proof that technology, when guided by experience and anchored by purpose, can amplify clarity without diluting conviction. The thinking remains human. The evidence remains real. The alignment remains intentional.

— *Andy Page Ph.D.*

www.ingramcontent.com/pod-product-compliance
Lightning Source LLC
Chambersburg PA
CBHW070204100426
42743CB00013B/3044